READY-TO-USE
LIBRARY SKILLS

Reproducible Activities for
Location and Literature Skills

Ruth V. Snoddon

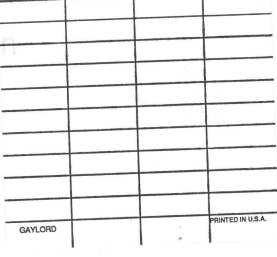

**THE CENTER FOR APPLIED
RESEARCH IN EDUCATION**
West Nyack, New York 10994

Library of Congress Cataloging-in-Publication Data

Snoddon, Ruth V.
    Ready-to-use library skills games.
    ISBN 0-87628-721-6
    1. School children—Library orientation.
  2. Elementary school libraries—Activity programs.
  3. Educational games. I. Title.
  Z675.S3S66 1987   86-23308
  025.5′678222   CIP

Printed in the United States of America

10 9 8 7 6 5

ISBN 0-87628-721-6

**THE CENTER FOR APPLIED RESEARCH
IN EDUCATION**
West Nyack, NY 10994

On the World Wide Web at http://www.phdirect.com

ABOUT THE AUTHOR

Ruth V. Snoddon, M.A., Northern Michigan University (Marquette), B.A., Laurentian University (Sudbury, Ontario), has been involved in elementary education for over twenty-five years as a classroom teacher and as a librarian. She has worked with curriculum committees, presented workshops on professional development, and compiled a policy manual for school library resource centers.

Mrs. Snoddon and Nancy M. Hall are the co-authors of *Guided Research Discovery Units*, a six-book series also published by The Center.

Contents

ABOUT *READY-TO-USE* *LIBRARY SKILLS GAMES*

Ready-to-Use Library Skills Games helps classroom teachers and library media specialists, grades 3–8, promote their students' interest in reading and the library media center, and teach or review functional library skills. The book consists of two games and twenty activities to build your students' location and literature skills.

DOOBY DEWEY

This game teaches the Dewey Decimal System. Played like bingo, Dooby Dewey consists of 35 different playing cards and 250 master squares of titles and their classifications. Dooby Dewey reinforces the idea that books on the same subject use the same classification letter or number. The Dooby Dewey game accomplishes the following objectives:

1. Familiarizes students with titles of children's books and their authors.
2. Familiarizes students with the Dewey Decimal System so that they will know that every book in the library has a specific place on the shelf.
3. Reinforces the fact that books on the same subject use the same classification letter or number.
4. Reinforces the fact that books with the same call number or letter are found in the same section of the library.
5. Reinforces the learning of commonly used classification numbers to which students can relate, such as 398.2 for fairy tales.

SUPER DOOBY

This game teaches about books, authors, the library, and the Dewey Decimal System. This is a library trivia game consisting of 480 questions and answers. The five categories (About Books, Authors, Dewey Decimal, Library Trivia, and Newbery Award Winners) familiarize your students with authors' names, characters in books, titles of books, the Dewey Decimal System, definitions and terms associated with the library, and Newbery Award winners. This game achieves the following:

1. Familiarizes students with authors and their books.
2. Reinforces knowledge and skills students have already acquired about authors and books.
3. Familiarizes students with characters found in books.
4. Reinforces knowledge and skills students have already acquired about characters in children's literature.
5. Familiarizes and reinforces knowledge about the ten Dewey Decimal classification divisions.
6. Familiarizes and reinforces knowledge pertaining to specific classification numbers for certain subjects of books within a class division.
7. Familiarizes and reinforces knowledge about authors, titles, dates, and characters associated with Newbery Award winners.
8. Familiarizes and reinforces knowledge students may have already acquired about terms and definitions relating to the library resource center.

ALPHA DOOBY FICTION ACTIVITIES

This section consists of ten sets of book spines that represent fiction books found on the library shelves. The sets are sequenced from easy to more difficult and reinforce arranging in alphabetical order by author's name and title of book. Alpha Dooby Fiction Activities provide practice in arranging:

1. Fiction books in alphabetical order according to author's last name, A–Z;
2. Fiction books in alphabetical order according to the second or third letter of the author's last name;
3. Fiction books in alphabetical order when there is more than one author with the same last name (the books are then arranged alphabetically by the author's first name);
4. Fiction books in order when more than one book is written by the same author (the books are then arranged alphabetically by the title of the book);
5. Fiction books in order by the second or third letters of the first word in some titles;
6. Fiction books in order by the second or third word in some titles;
7. Fiction books in order by the fourth, fifth, sixth, seventh, or eighth word in some titles;
8. Fiction books in order when the title of the book begins with "A," "An," or "The" (the books are then arranged alphabetically by the second word of the title).

ALPHA DOOBY NONFICTION ACTIVITIES

This section consists of ten sets of book spines that represent nonfiction books found on the library shelves. These sets are also sequenced from easy to more difficult and reinforce arranging books in order by the Dewey Decimal System, author's name, and title of book. These activities provide practice in arranging:

1. Nonfiction books in alphabetical order by the author's last name, A ·Z, with all books having the same call number;
2. Nonfiction books in alphabetical order by the author's last name, A–S, with books having the same call number;
3. Nonfiction books in alphabetical order by title of the book when there is more than one book by the same author, with all books having the same call number;
4. Nonfiction books in numerical order by different call numbers;
5. Nonfiction books in numerical order by different call numbers and decimal points;
6. Nonfiction books in numerical order by different call numbers, with some books arranged by the author's last name because of the same call number;
7. Biography books in order by the last name of the person the book is about;
8. Biography books in order by the last name of the person the book is about and by the author's last name when there is more than one book about the same person.

All of the activities in Sections Three and Four provide answer keys so that your students can check their own work. Simple rules for arranging books on the shelves have been provided along with reproducible bookends and directions for use in activity centers.

All of the games and activities in *Ready-to-Use Library Skills Games* can be reproduced as many times as needed to use with your students. They involve your students in the library center and give practice in crucial library skills. The games and activities also motivate your students, even those who may be turned off to library-oriented activities, by letting them have fun while they learn.

Ready-to-Use Library Skills Games provides activities that can be used all year to teach a variety of important library skills needed in the classroom, library, and any activity center. Use them and see how your students' interest in reading and the library grows and grows!

Ruth V. Snoddon

DOOBY DEWEY

A Game to Help Teach the Dewey Decimal System

DOOBY DEWEY

Game Objectives:

1. To familiarize students with titles of books and the Dewey Decimal System of classification used in a school library.
2. To reinforce the idea that books on the same subject, even though their titles differ, use the same classification number (call number). Therefore, books written on the same subject are located in the same section of the library. For example, *The True Book of Reptiles* and *A Book About Snakes* would both have the same call number and would both be on the same shelf.
3. To make working with the Dewey Decimal System more enjoyable.

Materials Needed:

- Tagboard
- Clear self-stick vinyl
- Scissors
- Glue
- Container
- *optional:* Plastic bingo markers

Construction Directions:

1. *Playing cards:* For a more permanent construction, glue the 35 playing cards onto tagboard. Cover them with clear self-stick vinyl and cut them out.
2. *Master squares:* Glue the pages containing the 250 master squares onto the tagboard and cover with self-stick vinyl. Cut out each square and place all the squares in a container. The 250 master squares are made up of the following book titles:

   D = 50 titles (includes Fiction and Religion—200s)

   E = 50 titles (includes 300s)

   W = 50 titles (includes 500s and 600s)

   E^2 = 50 titles (includes 700s and 800s)

   Y = 50 titles (includes 900s and Easy Reading)

3. *Markers:* Cut out enough 1" × 1" tagboard markers or use plastic bingo markers.

Playing Instructions:

1. Using any number of players from two to thirty-five, play Dooby Dewey just like bingo.
2. Each player must have a matching book title and call number (or call letter) before the square can be covered with a marker.

Uses:

- Dooby Dewey can be used with any class, small group, or library club (ages 8–14) familiar with the Dewey Decimal System.
- The game can be used as an introduction for teaching the Dewey Decimal System to students using a resource center.
- Dooby Dewey can be used to culminate lessons taught on the Dewey Decimal System.

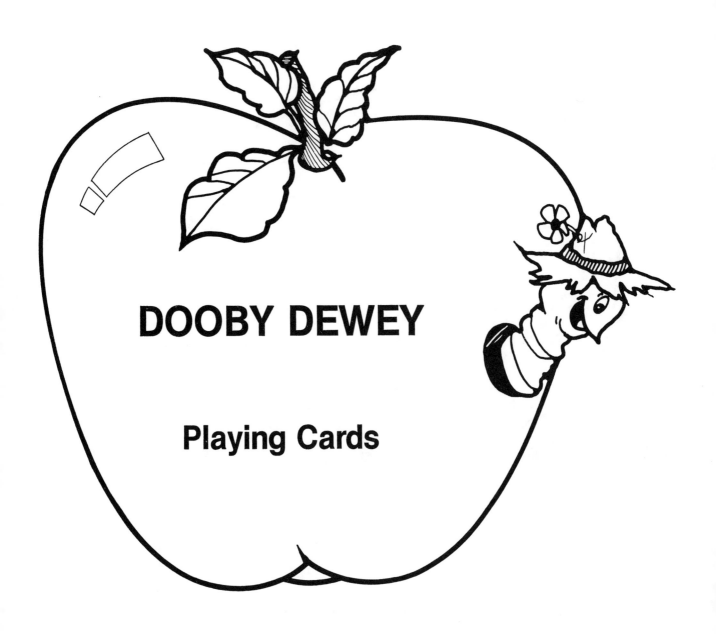

DOOBY DEWEY

Playing Cards

	D	E	W	E²	Y
D	F Away Goes Sally	398.2 Boy Who Cried Wolf	551.5 Snow	821.08 I Went to the Animal Fair	918 South America
O	220 Story of Moses	398.2 Emperor's New Clothes	551.3 First Book of Glaciers	745.5 Fun With Fabrics	921 Davy Crockett
O	F Adopted Jane	333.7 Wildlife in Danger		770 Fun With Your Camera	919.69 First Book of Hawaii
B	F Henry Huggins	398.2 Jack Tales	551.4 Story of Caves	745.5 Fun With Wire	910.9 Famous Modern Explorers
Y	F The Cave	333.7 First Book of Conservation	551.4 Tropical Rain Forests	745.5 Let's Make a Lot of Things	910.4 Book of Pirates

DEWEY

	D	E	W	E²	Y
D	291 Book of Myths	398.22 Robin Hood	551.4 Story of Caves	784 Canada's Story in Song	910.9 Famous Modern Explorers
O	F Blue Willow	371.42 I Want to Be a Doctor	523 The Sun	796.96 The Story of Hockey	916 All About Africa
O	220 Moses	398.2 Magic Listening Cap		730 How to Make Mobiles	E Secret Three
B	220 Children's Bible	398.22 Stories of King Arthur and His Knights	612 All About the Human Body	797.2 Swimming Book	917.9 Alaska
Y	F Happy Little Family	394.2 Night Before Christmas	576 Microbes at Work	821.08 Golden Treasury of Poetry	E Why I Built the Boogle House

D E W E² Y

	D	E	W	E²	Y
D	F Johnny Tremain	394.2 Night Before Christmas	510 New Ways in Math	793.7 Fun With Puzzles	910.92 Cartier Sails the St. Lawrence
O	292 Golden Fleece	398.2 Thumbelina	595.7 Bees and Wasps	738 Fun With Clay	915.4 India
O	F National Velvet	398.2 Paul Bunyan		745.5 Make It Yourself	E Theodore Turtle
B	F Twenty and Ten	394.2 Heigh-Ho for Halloween	551.5 Snow	745.5 Fun With Fabrics	948 First Book of Vikings
Y	F Homer Price	371.42 Vocations for Boys	597.8 Frogs and Toads	821 Peacock Pie	910.92 Man From St. Malo

DEWEY² DOOBY

	D	E	W	E²	Y
D	F Time Cat	398.2 Boy Who Cried Wolf	552 Story of Rocks	740 Pencil, Pen and Brush	910 Geography of the New World
O	F National Velvet	394.2 Harvest Feast	599 First Book of Mammals	793.7 Fun With Puzzles	921 Louisa May Alcott
O	291 Book of Myths	398.22 Robin Hood		745.5 Make It Yourself	948 First Book of Vikings
B	F Happy Little Family	398.8 Mother Goose	574 In Woods and Fields	738 Fun With Clay	971 Early Life in Canada
Y	F Baby Island	398.2 Princess of Tomboso	510 New Ways in Math	796.96 Hockey for Boys	910.92 Magellan

D	D	E	W	E²	Y
D	291 Book of Myths	398.2 Thunder in the Mountains	629.4 Rockets to the Moon	796.7 First and Fastest	E Millions of Cats
O	F Journey Cake	333.7 Wildlife in Danger	534 Magic of Sound	745.5 Make It Yourself	910.92 Cartier Sails the St. Lawrence
O	F Mine for Keeps	398.2 Three Billy Goats Gruff		738 Fun With Clay	E Timothy Turtle
B	F Snow Treasure	333.7 First Book of Conservation	529 First Book of Time	784 Complete Nursery Song Book	910.92 Captain of the Discovery
Y	F Rifles for Watie	394 Holidays Around the World	540.7 Experiments in Chemistry	821.08 Tom Tiddler's Ground	921 Davy Crockett

D	E	W	E²	Y
D F 39 Steps	398.2 Jack and the Beanstalk	636.7 Story of Dogs	796.96 The Story of Hockey	E Theodore Turtle
O 231 A Book About God	398.2 Which Was Witch?	581 First Book of Weeds	821 Complete Nonsense Book	E Red Fox and His Canoe
O F Away Goes Sally	398.2 Princess of Tomboso		821 Flint and Feather	973.7 Story of the Civil War
B 220 Old Testament	399 Warrior's Weapons	612 All About the Human Body	821.08 Tom Tiddler's Ground	E Dragon in the Clock Box
Y F Baby Island	395 Your Manners Are Showing	582 Backyard Trees	783 Sing for Christmas	971 Early Life in Canada

DEWEY

	D	E	W	E²	Y
D	220 Noah's Ark	384 Wonderful World of Communication	523 Big Dipper	709.98 Art of the Eskimo	921 Indian Captive
O	F Snow Treasure	398.2 Puss in Boots	591.5 Spike	793.7 Houseful of Laughter	E Happy Lion
O	F Adopted Jane	398.2 Boy Who Cried Wolf		821 Flint and Feather	971 Early Life in Canada
B	F Dolphin Boy	398.2 Tall Timber Tales	598.1 Turtles	745.5 Fun With Wire	910.92 Magellan
Y	F Wizard of Oz	398.2 Seven Ravens	550 What's Inside the Earth	709 Man Is an Artist	E Case of the Hungry Stranger

DEWEY DOOBY

	D	E	W	E²	Y
D	F Away Goes Sally	333.7 First Book of Conservation	537 What Is Electricity	796.96 Hockey for Boys	E Timothy Turtle
O	F Little Vic	394.2 Heigh-Ho for Halloween	582 Backyard Trees	797.2 Swimming Book	910.92 Man From St. Malo
O	220 Story of Moses	394 Holidays Around the World		821.08 Magic Circle	E Georgie
B	F Baby Island	398.2 Padre Porko	581 First Book of Weeds	821 Poems of Childhood	915.4 India
Y	F Big Red	398.2 Rapunzel	529 First Book of Time	821.08 I Went to the Animal Fair	917.2 Mexico

DOOBY — DEWE²Y

	D	E	W	E²	Y
D	F Little Women	398.2 Three Billy Goats Gruff	507 Fun With Science	821.08 Magic Circle	E Dragon in the Clock Box
O	F Dolphin Boy	359 Royal Navy	537 All About Electricity	796.96 The Story of Hockey	915.2 Young Japan
O	F Wizard of Oz	399 Warrior's Weapons		745.5 Make It and Use It	E Georgie
B	220 Children's Bible	398.2 Tall Timber Tales	523 Big Dipper	730 Clay, Wood and Wire	910.92 Cartier Sails the St. Lawrence
Y	F Journey Cake	398.2 Boy Who Cried Wolf	551.5 Lightning and Thunder	720 Study Book of Houses	921 Indian Captive

DEWEY DOOBY

D	E	W	E²	Y
D F The Borrowers	399 Warrior's Weapons	581 First Book of Weeds	770 Fun With Your Camera	E Millions of Cats
O 220 Story of Moses	398.2 Emperor's New Clothes	535 Light and Color	796.35 How to Play Baseball	910 Geography of the New World
O F Onion John	398.2 Seven Ravens		730 How to Make Mobiles	921 Louisa May Alcott
B 220 Children's Bible	398.2 Three Wishes	595.7 Bees and Wasps	793.7 Houseful of Laughter	919.69 First Book of Hawaii
Y F Baby Island	352 Scarlet Force	581 First Book of Wild Flowers	793.7 Fun With Puzzles	918 South America

D	E	W	E²	Y
F Twenty and Ten	387 Study Book of Ships	574 In Woods and Fields	821.08 Moon Is Shining Bright As Day	910.92 Captain of the Discovery
F Johnny Tremain	398.2 Magic Listening Cap	629.4 Rockets to the Moon	821.08 I Went to the Animal Fair	970.1 Indian Fishing and Camping
220 David	394.2 Christmas in Canada		797.2 Swimming Book	914.2 This Is London
292 Golden Fleece	398.2 Anansi, the Spider Man	551.4 Tropical Rain Forests	783 Sing for Christmas	973.7 Story of the Civil War
F The Cave	398.8 Mother Goose	599 First Book of Mammals	720 All the Ways of Building	E Red Fox and His Canoe

DOOBY

DEWEY DOOBY

	D	E	W	E²	Y
D	220 Noah's Ark	398.2 Which Was Witch?	523 Big Dipper	821.08 Magic	920 Great Names in Science
O	F Homer Price	398.2 Rapunzel	523 All About the Planets	720 All the Ways of Building	914.3 My Village in Austria
O	293 Thunder of the Gods	398.2 Thunder in the Mountains		796.35 How to Play Baseball	914.2 This Is London
B	F Adopted Jane	398.8 Land of Nursery Rhyme	537 What Is Electricity	821.08 Golden Treasury of Poetry	913 All About Archaeology
Y	F Blue Willow	394 Book of Holidays	581 Flowers	720 Look at Castles	948 First Book of Vikings

D	E	W	E²	Y
D 220 Story of Moses	398.2 Three Wishes	550 What's Inside the Earth	750 Famous Paintings	915.4 India
O F Happy Little Family	359 Royal Navy	636.7 Story of Dogs	709.32 Art of Ancient Egypt	910.92 Man From St. Malo
O 220 Ruth	352 Scarlett Force	*(free space)*	796.33 Football for Boys	E Secret Three
B F The Enormous Egg	395 Manners to Grow On	591 All About Whales	783 Sing for Christmas	910.9 Famous Modern Explorers
Y F Pinocchio	352 Police	582 Backyard Trees	709.98 Art of the Eskimo	910.92 Henry Hudson

Game board: **DEWEY²** (across top) / **DOOBY** (down left side)

	D	E	W	E²	Y
D	F Pinocchio	398.2 Christmas in Canada	599 First Book of Mammals	797.2 Swimming Book	E Little Leo
O	220 First Seven Days	371.42 I Want to Be a Ballet Dancer	529 First Book of Time	796.96 Hockey for Boys	914.97 My Village in Yugoslavia
O	F Little Vic	394 Holidays Around the World		740 Pencil, Pen and Brush	E Happy Lion
B	F Clue in Blue	395 Your Manners Are Showing	598.1 Turtles	745.5 Make It and Use It	E Theodore Turtle
Y	292 Greek Myths	398.2 Princess of Tomboso	598.1 Snakes	794.6 Bowling for Boys and Girls	910.4 Book of Pirates

DEWEY DOOBY

	D	E	W	E²	Y
D	F Journey Cake	394.2 Harvest Feast	574.92 Sea and Shore	709 Man Is an Artist	914.97 My Village in Yugoslavia
O	F Snow Treasure	394.2 Thanksgiving Story	574 Continent We Live On	745.5 Let's Make a Lot of Things	917.1 Made in Canada
O	F Mine for Keeps	394.2 Christmas in Canada		821 Complete Nonsense Book	E Little Leo
B	F Rifles for Watie	398.2 Pecos Bill	551.4 Story of Caves	796.5 Wildwood Wisdom	E Happy Lion
Y	F Little Pear	384 Wonderful World of Communication	574 In Woods and Fields	720 Houses	E Theodore Turtle

DEWEY DOOBY

	D	E	W	E²	Y
D	F Clue in Blue	395 Manners to Grow On	599 First Book of Mammals	821.08 I Went to the Animal Fair	E Billy and Blaze
O	220 David	398.2 Anansi, the Spider Man	552 Story of Rocks	797.2 Swimming Book	E Wee Gillis
O	F Johnny Tremain	398.22 Robin Hood		822.3 Tales from Shakespeare	940.1 Made in the Middle Ages
B	220 First Seven Days	394.2 Thanksgiving Story	574 In Woods and Fields	796.33 Football for Boys	910.92 Captain of the Discovery
Y	F Pinocchio	398.8 Lavender's Blue	597.8 Frogs and Toads	730 Clay, Wood and Wire	915.2 Japan

D	E	W	E²	Y
D	F Madeline Takes Command	371.42 I Want to Be a Ballet Dancer	551.4 Tropical Rain Forests	709.67 Art of the North American Indian	E Billy and Blaze
O	220 Moses	387 Study Book of Ships	574.92 Goldfish	821 Now We Are Six	E Mike's House
O	F Mouse House	398.2 Thumbelina		793.7 Fun With Puzzles	E Little Leo
B	220 Ruth	394 Holidays Around the World	581 How a Seed Grows	796.7 First and Fastest	917.9 Alaska
Y	F Little Vic	395 Your Manners Are Showing	576 Microbes at Work	750 Famous Paintings	920 Great Names in Science

DEWEY² DOOBY

	D	E	W	E²	Y
D	220 Ruth	398.2 Jack and the Beanstalk	612 All About the Human Body	793.7 Fun With Puzzles	917.1 Canada
O	F Little Pear	398.2 Cinderella	539 All About the Atom	709.67 Art of the North American Indian	914.2 This Is London
O	291 Book of Myths	394.2 Thanksgiving Story		784 Canada's Story in Song	E Happy Lion
B	F Happy Little Family	394.2 Heigh-Ho for Halloween	523 The Sun	821 Hailstones and Halibut Bones	914.3 My Village in Austria
Y	F Big Red	371.42 Vocations for Boys	612 Your Eyes	720 Houses	910.92 Henry Hudson

WEST BRIDGEWATER PUBLIC LIBRARY
80 Howard Street
West Bridgewater, MA 02379

DEWEY DOOBY

	D	E	W	E²	Y
D	F Wizard of Oz	387 Oars, Sails and Steam	591 Camels and Llamas	821 Poems of Childhood	910 Geography of the New World
O	220 Noah's Ark	394.2 Heigh-Ho for Halloween	523 All About the Planets	822.3 Tales From Shakespeare	919.69 First Book of Hawaii
O	F National Velvet	394 Book of Holidays		796.33 Football for Boys	E Timothy Turtle
B	F Twenty and Ten	398.2 Pecos Bill	591.5 Spike	709.38 Art of Ancient Rome	970.1 Indian Fishing and Camping
Y	F Coral Island	387 Study Book of Ships	591 Animals in Winter	720 Study Book of Houses	917.1 Canada

DEWEY DOOBY

D	E	W	E²	Y
F — Clue in Blue	**359** — Royal Navy	**598.1** — Turtles	**784** — Canada's Story in Song	**921** — Davy Crockett
F — Coral Island	**395** — Your Manners Are Showing	**595.7** — Little Black Ant	**821.08** — Moon Is Shining Bright As Day	**915.2** — Young Japan
F — Little Women	**371.42** — I Want to Be a Farmer		**784** — Complete Nursery Song Book	**971** — Early Life in Canada
220 — Noah's Ark	**398.22** — Stories of King Arthur and His Knights	**591** — Camels and Llamas	**796.7** — First and Fastest	**914.97** — My Village in Yugoslavia
220 — Joseph and His Brothers	**371.42** — I Want to Be a Nurse	**591.5** — Spike	**783** — Sing for Christmas	**973.7** — Story of the Civil War

DEWEY

	D	E	W	E²	Y
D	F Madeline Takes Command	394.2 Night Before Christmas	598.2 Ostriches	821 Peacock Pie	E Little Leo
O	F The Ark	387 Oars, Sails and Steam	523 The Sun	709.98 Art of the Eskimo	E Mike's House
O	220 David	394.2 Harvest Feast	*(free space)*	821.08 My Poetry Book	918 South America
B	F Clue in Blue	384 Wonderful World of Communication	598.2 Birds and Their Nests	796.32 Volleyball	910.4 Book of Pirates
Y	F Twenty and Ten	394.2 Thanksgiving Story	595.7 Little Black Ant	730 Clay, Wood and Wire	919.69 First Book of Hawaii

DEWEY DOOBY

	D	E	W	E²	Y
D	F The Ark	398.2 Cinderella	551.5 All About the Weather	720 Look at Castles	948 First Book of Vikings
O	F Prairie School	398.22 Stories of King Arthur and His Knights	581 First Book of Wild Flowers	750 Famous Paintings	913 All About Archaeology
O	220 Old Testament	398.2 Rapunzel		709.98 Art of Ancient Rome	E Three to Get Ready
B	F Coral Island	371.42 I Want to Be a Ballet Dancer	581 Flowers	821 Hailstones and Halibut Bones	E Case of the Hungry Stranger
Y	220 Joseph and His Brothers	398.2 Three Billy Goats Gruff	591 All About Whales	720 Houses	910.92 Columbus

	D	E	W	E²	Y
D	220 Children's Bible	398.2 Which Was Witch?	552 Story of Rocks	796.32 Volleyball	914.92 Land and People of Holland
O	F Time Cat	398.8 Lavender's Blue	540.7 Experiments in Chemistry	793.8 Magic Made Easy	910.92 Magellan
O	292 Greek Myths	371.42 I Want to Be an Engineer		821 Now We Are Six	920 Great Names in Science
B	F Prairie School	398.8 Jack Tales	507 Fun With Science	796.5 Wildwood Wisdom	E Wee Gillis
Y	F Wizard of Oz	352 Police	534 Magic of Sound	821 Complete Nonsense Book	940.1 Made in the Middle Ages

DEWEY — **DOOBY**

	D	E	W	E²	Y
D	F The Borrowers	398.2 Pecos Bill	540.7 Experiments in Chemistry	796.5 Wildwood Wisdom	E Three to Get Ready
O	F Onion John	352 Scarlet Force	568 Prehistoric Animals	821 Now We Are Six	910.92 Columbus
O	F Henry Huggins	398.2 Padre Porko		821 Poems of Childhood	910.92 Henry Hudson
B	F Time Cat	352 Police	597.7 Little Black Ant	821.08 My Poetry Book	970.1 Indian Fishing and Camping
Y	F The Cave	398.2 Cinderella	507 Fun With Science	821.08 Tom Tiddler's Ground	921 Davy Crockett

DEWE²Y

D	E	W	E²	Y
220 Moses	398.2 Three Wishes	551.4 Story of Caves	821.08 Tom Tiddler's Ground	914.3 My Village in Austria
293 Thunder of the Gods	398.22 Stories of King Arthur and His Knights	552 Story of Rocks	822.3 Tales From Shakespeare	910.92 Magellan
F 39 Steps	371.42 I Want to Be a Farmer		796.33 Football for Boys	910.92 Captain of the Discovery
F Twenty-one Balloons	394.2 Christmas in Canada	568 All About Dinosaurs	793.7 Fun With Puzzles	971 Early Life in Canada
F The Enormous Egg	398.8 Lavender's Blue	523 Big Dipper	730 Clay, Wood and Wire	916 All About Africa

D O O B Y

	D	E²	W	E	Y
D	F Little Women	398.2 Jack Tales	551.5 Lightning and Thunder	821.08 Moon Is Shining Bright As Day	E Georgie
O	231 A Book About God	398.2 Thunder in the Mountains	537 All About Electricity	784 Complete Nursery Song Book	E Dragon in the Clock Box
O	F Mine for Keeps	371.42 I Want to Be a Doctor		821 Now We Are Six	914.81 Arne of Norway
B	F 39 Steps	398.2 Seven Ravens	591 Animals in Winter	709.38 Art of Ancient Greece	E Red Fox and His Canoe
Y	F Prairie School	398.2 Stone Soup	591 All About Whales	745.5 Let's Make a Lot of Things	E Wee Gillis

DEWEY DOOBY

	D	E	W	E²	Y
D	293 Thunder of the Gods	333.7 Wildlife in Danger	629.4 Rockets to the Moon	821 Complete Nonsense Book	970.1 Indian Fishing and Camping
O	F The Enormous Egg	398.2 Jack and the Beanstalk	568 Dinosaurs	709.32 Art of Ancient Egypt	973.7 Story of the Civil War
O	F Rifles for Watie	399 Warrior's Weapons		796.32 Volleyball	E Millions of Cats
B	F Journey Cake	398.2 Which Was Witch?	574.92 Sea and Shore	796.35 How to Play Baseball	921 Indian Captive
Y	F Half Magic	398.2 Tall Timber Tales	591 Camels and Llamas	720 All the Ways of Building	914.5 Life in Europe: Italy

D O O B Y — D E W E² Y

	D	E	W	E²	Y
D	F Rifles for Watie	395 Manners to Grow On	537 What Is Electricity	821.08 My Poetry Book	E Why I Built the Boogle House
O	F Half Magic	394 Book of Holidays	568 All About Dinosaurs	783 Sing for Christmas	915.2 Japan
O	F Twenty-one Balloons	371.42 I Want to Be an Engineer		745.5 Fun With Fabrics	E Mike's House
B	F Adopted Jane	398.2 Emperor's New Clothes	537 All About Electricity	784 Complete Nursery Song Book	E Secret Three
Y	F Madeline Takes Command	371.42 I Want to Be a Nurse	551.5 All About the Weather	784 Canada's Story in Song	E Red Fox and His Canoe

DEWEY

DOOBY

	D	E	W	E²	Y
D	F Big Red	387 Oars, Sails and Steam	568 Prehistoric Animals	793.8 Magic Made Easy	913 All About Archaeology
O	291 Book of Myths	394.2 Night Before Christmas	568 Dinosaurs	821.08 Golden Treasury of Poetry	914.92 Land and People of Holland
O	F Onion John	398.2 Stone Soup		745.5 Fun With Wire	916 All About Africa
B	F Happy Little Family	333.7 Wildlife in Danger	551.5 Snow	822.3 Tales From Shakespeare	E Why I Built the Boogle House
Y	F Blue Willow	394 Book of Holidays	535 Light and Color	796.35 How to Play Baseball	910.9 Famous Modern Explorers

DEWEY DOOBY

	D	E	W	E²	Y
D	292 The Odyssey	395 Manners to Grow On	551.3 First Book of Glaciers	821 Poems of Childhood	E Red Fox and His Canoe
O	F Homer Price	398.2 Paul Bunyan	598.2 Birds and Their Nests	709.38 Art of Ancient Greece	917.2 Mexico
O	F Twenty-one Balloons	398.2 Princess of Tomboso		796.96 Hockey for Boys	921 Indian Captive
B	292 Greek Myths	398.2 Magic Listening Cap	574.92 Goldfish	740 Paper, Ink and Roller	917.1 Made in Canada
Y	F Blue Willow	398.2 Puss in Boots	523 All About the Planets	821 Flint and Feather	917.9 Alaska

DEWEY

	D	E	W	E²	Y
D	292 The Odyssey	398.2 Jack Tales	523 Big Dipper	709.38 Art of Ancient Greece	940.1 Made in the Middle Ages
O	F Madeline Takes Command	371.42 I Want to Be a Nurse	568 All About Dinosaurs	740 Paper, Ink and Roller	E Timothy Turtle
O	220 First Seven Days	398.2 Magic Listening Cap		745.5 Make It Yourself	E Millions of Cats
B	F Pinocchio	371.42 I Want to Be a Ballet Dancer	507 Fun With Science	821.08 Moon Is Shining Bright As Day	910.92 Cartier Sails the St. Lawrence
Y	220 Moses	395 Manners to Grow On	551.4 Story of Caves	794.6 Bowling for Boys and Girls	910.92 Man From St. Malo

	D	E	W	E²	Y
D	220 Joseph and His Brothers	398.2 Anansi, the Spider Man	574 The Continent We Live On	821.08 Golden Treasury of Poetry	915.2 Japan
O	F Johnny Tremain	394.2 Harvest Feast	612 Your Eyes	796.96 The Story of Hockey	914.81 Arne of Norway
O	F Homer Price	371.42 I Want to Be A Farmer		750 Famous Paintings	910.92 Henry Hudson
B	F The Enormous Egg	398.2 Paul Bunyan	598.1 Snakes	720 Look at Castles	E Wee Gillis
Y	F The Borrowers	398.2 Cinderella	568 All About Dinosaurs	709.38 Art of Ancient Rome	917.1 Canada

DEWEY
DOOBY

	D	E	W	E²	Y
D	F The Ark	394.2 Harvest Feast	591 Animals in Winter	709.32 Art of Ancient Egypt	E Georgie
O	292 Golden Fleece	394 Book of Holidays	598.1 Snakes	745.5 Fun With Wire	E Dragon in the Clock Box
O	F National Velvet	398.2 Emperor's New Clothes		796.5 Wildwood Wisdom	921 Louisa May Alcott
B	220 David	398.8 Land of Nursery Rhyme	535 Light and Color	745.5 Fun With Fabrics	915.2 Japan
Y	220 Old Testament	398.2 Three Wishes	581 How a Seed Grows	794.6 Bowling for Boys and Girls	914.92 Land and People of Holland

	D	E	W	E²	Y
D	F Snow Treasure	398.8 Mother Goose	591.5 Spike	821.08 My Poetry Book	910.92 Columbus
O	220 First Seven Days	398.2 Cinderella	598.2 Ostriches	720 Look at Castles	915.2 Japan
O	F Johnny Tremain	399 Warrior's Weapons		797.2 Swimming Book	921 Indian Captive
B	220 Story of Moses	352 Scarlet Force	591 All About Whales	796.7 First and Fastest	973.7 Story of the Civil War
Y	293 Thunder of the Gods	398.2 Boy Who Cried Wolf	523 Big Dipper	821 Now We Are Six	E Happy Lion

DEWEY

D	E	W	E²	Y
D 292 The Odyssey	398.8 Land of Nursery Rhyme	534 Magic of Sound	770 Fun With Your Camera	920 Great Names in Science
O F Time Cat	398.8 Mother Goose	629.4 Rockets to the Moon	783 Sing for Christmas	921 Louisa May Alcott
O F The Cave	371.42 Vocations for Boys		793.8 Magic Made Easy	914.81 Arne of Norway
B 293 Thunder of the Gods	394.2 Heigh-Ho for Halloween	552 Rocks and Gems	821.08 My Poetry Book	917.2 Mexico
Y F Little Women	398.8 Lavender's Blue	595.7 Bees and Wasps	821 Hailstones and Halibut Bones	914.5 Life in Europe: Italy

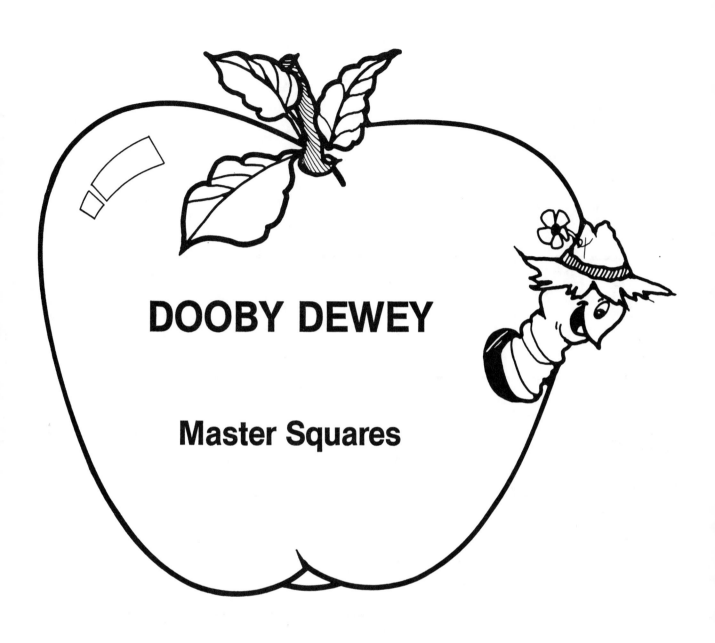

DOOBY DEWEY

Master Squares

D	D	D	D	D
F Adopted Jane	F The Ark	F Away Goes Sally	F Baby Island	F Big Red
D	D	D	D	D
F Blue Willow	F The Borrowers	F The Cave	F Clue in Blue	F Coral Island
D	D	D	D	D
F Dolphin Boy	F The Enormous Egg	F Half Magic	F Happy Little Family	F Henry Huggins
D	D	D	D	D
F Homer Price	F Johnny Tremain	F Journey Cake	F Little Pear	F Little Vic
D	D	D	D	D
F Little Women	F Madeline Takes Command	F Mine for Keeps	F Mouse House	F National Velvet

D F Onion John	D F Pinocchio	D F Prairie School	D F Rifles for Watie	D F Snow Treasure
D F 39 Steps	D F Time Cat	D F Twenty and Ten	D F Twenty-one Balloons	D F Wizard of Oz
D 220 Children's Bible	D 220 David	D 220 First Seven Days	D 220 Joseph and His Brothers	D 220 Moses
D 220 Noah's Ark	D 220 Old Testament	D 220 Ruth	D 220 Story of Moses	D 220 A Book About God
D 291 Book of Myths	D 292 Golden Fleece	D 292 Greek Myths	D 292 The Odyssey	D 293 Thunder of the Gods

E	E	E	E	E
333.7 First Book of Conservation	333.7 Wildlife in Danger	352 Police	352 Scarlet Force	359 Royal Navy
371.42 I Want to Be a Ballet Dancer	371.42 I Want to Be a Doctor	371.42 I Want to Be a Farmer	371.42 I Want to Be a Nurse	371.42 I Want to Be an Engineer
371.42 Vocations for Boys	384 Wonderful World of Communication	387 Oars, Sails, and Steam	387 Study Book of Ships	394 Book of Holidays
394 Holidays Around the World	394.2 Christmas in Canada	394.2 Harvest Feast	394.2 Heigh-Ho for Halloween	394.2 Night Before Christmas
394.2 Thanksgiving Story	395 Manners to Grow On	395 Your Manners Are Showing	398.2 Anansi, the Spider Man	398.2 Boy Who Cried Wolf

E 398.2 Cinderella	E 398.2 Emperor's New Clothes	E 398.2 Jack and the Beanstalk	E 398.2 Jack Tales	E 398.2 Magic Listening Cap
E 398.2 Padre Porko	E 398.2 Paul Bunyan	E 398.2 Pecos Bill	E 398.2 Princess of Tomboso	E 398.2 Puss in Boots
E 398.2 Rapunzel	E 398.2 Seven Ravens	E 398.2 Stone Soup	E 398.2 Tall Timber Tales	E 398.2 Three Billy Goats Gruff
E 398.2 Three Wishes	E 398.2 Thumbelina	E 398.2 Thunder in the Mountains	E 398.2 Which Was Witch?	E 398.22 Robin Hood
E 398.22 Stories of King Arthur and His Knights	E 398.8 Land of Nursery Rhyme	E 398.8 Lavender's Blue	E 398.8 Mother Goose	E 399 Warrior's Weapons

W 507 Fun With Science	W 510 New Ways in Math	W 523 All About the Planets	W 523 Big Dipper	W 523 The Sun
W 529 First Book of Time	W 534 Magic of Sound	W 535 Light and Color	W 537 All About Electricity	W 537 What Is Electricity
W 539 All About the Atom	W 540.7 Experiments in Chemistry	W 550 What's Inside the Earth	W 551.3 First Book of Glaciers	W 551.4 Story of Caves
W 551.4 Tropical Rain Forests	W 551.5 All About the Weather	W 551.5 Lightning and Thunder	W 551.5 Snow	W 552 Rocks and Gems
W 552 Story of Rocks	W 568 All About Dinosaurs	W 568 Dinosaurs	W 568 Prehistoric Animals	W 574 The Continent We Live On

W 574 In Woods and Fields	W 574.92 Goldfish	W 574.92 Sea and Shore	W 576 Microbes at Work	W 581 First Book of Weeds
W 581 First Book of Wild Flowers	W 581 Flowers	W 581 How a Seed Grows	W 582 Backyard Trees	W 591 All About Whales
W 591 Animals in Winter	W 591 Camels and Llamas	W 591.5 Spike	W 595.7 Bees and Wasps	W 595.7 Little Black Ant
W 597.8 Frogs and Toads	W 598.1 Snakes	W 598.1 Turtles	W 598.2 Birds and Their Nests	W 598.2 Ostriches
W 599 First Book of Mammals	W 612 All About the Human Body	W 612 Your Eyes	W 629.4 Rockets to the Moon	W 636.7 Story of Dogs

E² 709.32 Art of Ancient Egypt	E² 709.38 Art of Ancient Greece	E² 709.38 Art of Ancient Rome	E² 709.98 Art of the Eskimo	E² 709.67 Art of the North American Indian
E² 709 Man Is an Artist	E² 720 All the Ways of Building	E² 720 Houses	E² 720 Look at Castles	E² 720 Study Book of Houses
E² 730 Clay, Wood and Wire	E² 730 How to Make Mobiles	E² 738 Fun With Clay	E² 740 Paper, Ink and Roller	E² 740 Pencil, Pen and Brush
E² 745.5 Fun With Fabrics	E² 745.5 Fun With Wire	E² 745.5 Let's Make a Lot of Things	E² 745.5 Make It and Use It	E² 745.5 Make It Yourself
E² 750 Famous Paintings	E² 770 Fun With Your Camera	E² 783 Sing for Christmas	E² 784 Canada's Story in Song	E² 784 Complete Nursery Song Book

E² 793.7 Fun With Puzzles	E² 793.7 Houseful of Laughter	E² 793.8 Magic Made Easy	E² 794.6 Bowling for Boys and Girls	E² 796.32 Volleyball
E² 796.33 Football for Boys	E² 796.35 How to Play Baseball	E² 796.5 Wildwood Wisdom	E² 796.7 First and Fastest	E² 796.96 Hockey for Boys
E² 796.96 The Story of Hockey	E² 797.2 Swimming Book	E² 821 Complete Nonsense Book	E² 821 Flint and Feather	E² 821 Hailstones and Halibut Bones
E² 821 Now We Are Six	E² 821 Peacock Pie	E² 821 Poems of Childhood	E² 821.08 Golden Treasury of Poetry	E² 821.08 I Went to the Animal Fair
E² 821.08 Magic Circle	E² 821.08 Moon Is Shining Bright As Day	E² 821.08 My Poetry Book	E² 821.08 Tom Tiddler's Ground	E² 822.3 Tales From Shakespeare

Y	Y	Y	Y	Y
E Billy and Blaze	E Case of the Hungry Stranger	E Dragon in the Clock Box	E Georgie	E Happy Lion
Y	Y	Y	Y	Y
E Little Leo	E Mike's House	E Millions of Cats	E Red Fox and His Canoe	E Secret Three
Y	Y	Y	Y	Y
E Theodore Turtle	E Three to Get Ready	E Timothy Turtle	E Wee Gillis	E Why I Built the Boogle House
Y	Y	Y	Y	Y
910 Geography of the New World	910.4 Book of Pirates	910.9 Famous Modern Explorers	910.92 Captain of the Discovery	910.92 Cartier Sails the St. Lawrence
Y	Y	Y	Y	Y
910.92 Columbus	910.92 Henry Hudson	910.92 Magellan	910.92 Man From St. Malo	913 All About Archaeology

Y 914.2 This Is London	Y 914.3 My Village in Austria	Y 914.5 Life in Europe: Italy	Y 914.81 Arne of Norway	Y 914.92 Land and People of Holland
Y 914.97 My Village in Yugoslavia	Y 915.2 Japan	Y 915.2 Young Japan	Y 915.4 India	Y 916 All About Africa
Y 917.1 Canada	Y 917.1 Made in Canada	Y 917.2 Mexico	Y 917.9 Alaska	Y 918 South America
Y 919.69 First Book of Hawaii	Y 920 Great Names in Science	Y 921 Louisa May Alcott	Y 921 Davy Crockett	Y 921 Indian Captive
Y 940.1 Made in the Middle Ages	Y 948 First Book of Vikings	Y 970.1 Indian Fishing and Camping	Y 971 Early Life in Canada	Y 973.7 Story of the Civil War

SUPER DOOBY

A Game to Teach About Books, Authors, the Library, and the Dewey Decimal System

SUPER DOOBY

Games Objectives:

1. To familiarize students with authors' names, characters in books, titles of books, the Dewey Decimal System, Newbery Award-winning titles, and definitions and terms associated with the library.

2. To reinforce the skills and knowledge students acquire through use of books and a library media center.

3. To approach library-centered knowledge in an interesting, informative, and enjoyable way.

Materials Needed:

- Clear self-stick vinyl
- Container
- Scissors
- *optional:* Glue
- *optional:* Tagboard

Construction Directions:

1. *Playing cards:* For a more permanent construction, glue the 40 pages containing the questions for each of the five categories onto tagboard. Cover them with clear self-stick vinyl and cut out the six cards on each page. You will then have 48 cards for each category.

2. *Players' Scores:* Make as many copies of this score sheet as you need.

Playing Instructions for Individuals:

1. Super Dooby consists of 480 questions with 96 questions in each of the following categories: About Books, Authors, Dewey Decimal, Library Trivia, and Newbery Awards. The first question on each card is worth one point, and the second question is worth two points if answered correctly.

2. The first player to reach a total of 20 points wins the game. In reaching this total, a player must get at least two points in each of the five categories, but not more than five points in any one category. If time does not allow any player to attain 20 points, the person with the most points when the game is concluded will be named winner.

3. Select a "quiz master" who will record the score on the players' score card and monitor the play. For example, this person will put a "1" or "2" under the correct category when a player answers a question correctly and will also inform any person who has received five points under any one category. The "quiz master" will also keep a running total of each player's points.

4. The sets of cards can be distributed among the players so that more than one person asks the questions or, if desired, one person may be in charge of calling out questions when a player has requested the category and

question number he or she wants to answer. The person calling out the question takes it from the top of the pile and then places it at the bottom when the question has been called.

5. Shuffle the cards before play begins. Any player can begin the game. Play will then pass to the player on the left of the previous player and continue in a clockwise direction. Each player answers only *one* question at each turn, regardless of whether the answer is correct or not.

6. When a player is claimed winner, play continues until the round is completed so that each player has been given the same number of questions. If another player ties, the people involved will be given a tie-breaking question by the "quiz master" in the categories of their choice.

Playing Instructions for Teams:

1. Teams may be formed when four or more players are involved. Players may choose how the team operates; however, only the first answer given from each team will be accepted.

2. Points are earned as a team and scored accordingly.

Uses:

- Super Dooby can be used with any class, small group, or library club familiar with books, authors, the Dewey Decimal System, and library terminology.
- The game can be used to motivate students to learn more about the five categories played.
- Super Dooby can also be used in a library, a classroom, or any activity center.

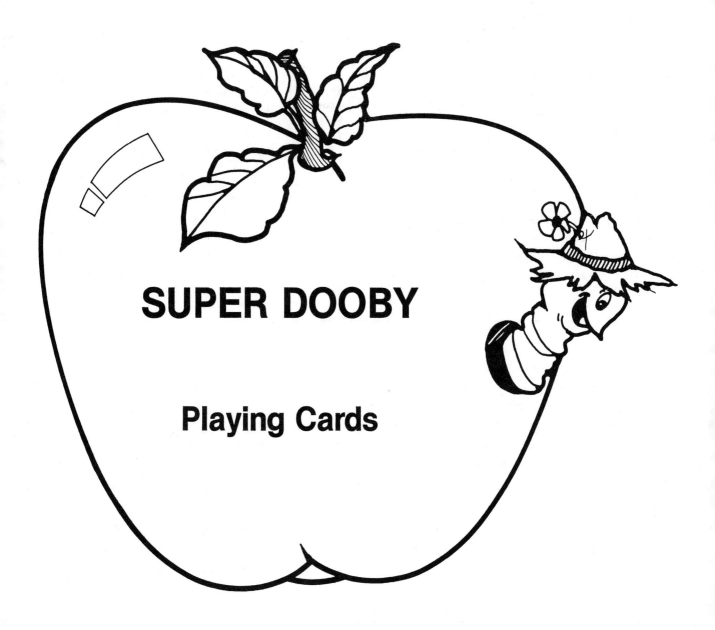

SUPER DOOBY

Playing Cards

ABOUT BOOKS

ABOUT BOOKS

1. What is Johnny Appleseed known for?
2. *Sister of the Bride* and *Runaway Ralph* are two books written by this author.

————

1. Planting apple trees as he traveled.
2. Beverly Cleary.

ABOUT BOOKS

1. Who was Old Yeller in the book by the same name?
2. When the wife hummed in the book *Sounder*, what did this mean?

————

1. A dog.
2. She was worried.

ABOUT BOOKS

1. In what state was Abe Lincoln born?
2. A lost diamond bracelet is an important part of this story written by Robert McCloskey.

————

1. Kentucky.
2. *Homer Price.*

ABOUT BOOKS

1. Who was Harriet Tubman?
2. Jamie, Awasin, and Angus MacNair are characters in this book.

————

1. Negro slave who helped set her people free.
2. *Lost in the Barrens*, or *Two Against the North*

ABOUT BOOKS

1. What was Mike Fink known for?
2. *Tex* and *Rumble Fish* are two books written by this author.

————

1. Boatman on the Mississippi.
2. S.E. Hinton.

ABOUT BOOKS

1. What family landed on a deserted island in 1704?
2. Name the two children who tried to tame Misty of Chincoteague.

————

1. Swiss Family Robinson.
2. Paul and Maureen.

ABOUT BOOKS

ABOUT BOOKS

1. He slept for 20 years.
2. In the book *Mouse and the Motorcycle* by Cleary, what was Ralph's favorite sandwich?

_____

1. Rip Van Winkle.
2. Peanut butter and jelly.

ABOUT BOOKS

1. This author wrote books about Henry Huggins, Ribsy, and Ramona.
2. *Homer Price, Time of Wonder,* and *One Morning in Maine* are three books written by this author.

_____

1. Beverly Cleary.
2. Robert McCloskey.

ABOUT BOOKS

1. Miss Turner, Professor, Falcon, and Sam Gribley are characters in this book.
2. Robert Heinlein is noted for writing what certain kind of book?

_____

1. *My Side of the Mountain.*
2. Science fiction.

ABOUT BOOKS

1. What kind of boats did the people ride on in the book *Mark Twain*?
2. *Organdy Cupcakes, Wait for Me, Michael,* and *Who Wants Music on Monday* are three of her books.

_____

1. Steamboats.
2. Mary Stolz.

ABOUT BOOKS

1. In what book does a pig named Wilbur try to fly?
2. When Betsy Ross died, who was president of the United States?

_____

1. *Charlotte's Web.*
2. Andrew Jackson.

ABOUT BOOKS

1. *Call of the Wild* and *White Fang* are two of the books he wrote.
2. What was Mark Twain's real name?

_____

1. Jack London.
2. Samuel Clemens.

ABOUT BOOKS

ABOUT BOOKS
1. This writer created the Moffats.
2. *Durango Street, Nitty Gritty*, and *Mystery of the Fat Cat* are three of his books.

———

1. Eleanor Estes.
2. Frank Bonham.

ABOUT BOOKS
1. What was Pegasus in Greek mythology?
2. *Going on Sixteen, Jenny Kimura*, and *Accent on April* are three of her books.

———

1. A winged horse.
2. Betty Cavanna.

ABOUT BOOKS
1. For what was Pecos Bill most famous?
2. Lorraine, John, Mr. Pignate, and Bobo are characters in this book.

———

1. Cowboy or cowpuncher.
2. *The Pigman.*

ABOUT BOOKS
1. For what is John Henry known?
2. Dennis, Liz, Maggie, and Sean are characters in this book.

———

1. Railroad builder or driving steel.
2. *My Darling, My Hamburger.*

ABOUT BOOKS
1. Of whom was Jason, a character in Greek mythology, leader?
2. *Letters to a Teen-age Son, Street Rods*, and *Hot Rod* are three of his books.

———

1. Argonauts.
2. Henry Felsen.

ABOUT BOOKS
1. Who was Aphrodite in Greek mythology?
2. *Indian Captive, Puritan Girl*, and *Cotton in My Sack* are three of her books.

———

1. Goddess of love and beauty.
2. Lois Lenski.

ABOUT BOOKS

1. In what type of work was Paul Bunyan outstanding?
2. Books such as *The Pigman, I Never Loved Your Mind,* and *My Darling, My Hamburger* are written by this author.

———

1. Lumberjack.
2. Paul Zindel.

ABOUT BOOKS

1. She is the Canadian author of *Incredible Journey,* an exciting animal adventure tale.
2. In what war did Florence Nightingale take part?

———

1. Sheila Burnford.
2. Crimean War.

ABOUT BOOKS

1. Who is the main character of *Born Free* by Joy Adamson?
2. In the book *Beezus and Ramona,* what is Beezus' real name?

———

1. Elsa, the lion.
2. Beatrice Quimby.

ABOUT BOOKS

1. This author wrote *Winnie the Pooh* and *When We Were Very Young.*
2. In the book *Tales of a Fourth Grade Nothing,* what was Peter Hatcher's little brother's real name?

———

1. A.A. Milne.
2. Farley Drexel Hatcher.

ABOUT BOOKS

1. *Little House in the Big Woods* and *Farmer Boy* are two books written by this author.
2. Name the teen-ager who gets inside the world of jazz in *Jazz Country* by Nat Hentoff.

———

1. Laura Ingalls Wilder.
2. Tom.

ABOUT BOOKS

1. In the book *Tales of a Fourth Grade Nothing,* what did Peter name his pet turtle?
2. What religion was Betsy Ross' family?

———

1. Dribble.
2. Quaker.

ABOUT BOOKS

ABOUT BOOKS

1. Who is Lassie in the book *Lassie Come-Home* by Eric Knight?
2. Who was the president of the country when Jim Thorpe died on March 28, 1953?

———

1. A dog.
2. Dwight D. Eisenhower.

ABOUT BOOKS

1. What did Casey Jones like to ride?
2. In the book *Anne of Green Gables*, who was the boy that called Anne carrots?

———

1. A train.
2. Gilbert Blythe.

ABOUT BOOKS

1. In the book *Henry Huggins*, why is the dog's name Ribsy?
2. This author wrote many U.S. regional stories.

———

1. He was so thin you could see his ribs.
2. Lois Lenski.

ABOUT BOOKS

1. Marguerite Henry is noted for writing many stories about this animal.
2. Alicia, Bo Jo, Julie, and Mary are characters in this book.

———

1. Horse.
2. *Mr. and Mrs. Bo Jo Jones.*

ABOUT BOOKS

1. In the book *Old Yeller*, who was Old Yeller's master?
2. Fabulous diamond mines were written about in this Newbery Award winner.

———

1. Travis.
2. *Twenty-one Balloons.*

ABOUT BOOKS

1. This author wrote stories about Mary Poppins.
2. In the book *Alice in Wonderland*, what did Alice find on the table?

———

1. P.L. Travers.
2. A bottle with the words "Drink Me."

ABOUT BOOKS

ABOUT BOOKS

1. He is the author of *The Legend of Sleepy Hollow.*
2. His pen name was Mark Twain and his books, though not new, are still popular.

———

1. Washington Irving.
2. Samuel Clemens.

ABOUT BOOKS

1. What did Icarus do in a Greek mythology story?
2. Helen, Annie Sullivan, Kate Keller, and Captain Keller are characters in this play.

———

1. He flew too close to the sun.
2. *The Miracle Worker.*

ABOUT BOOKS

1. His "Peanuts" characters appear daily in many newspapers as well as in books.
2. Charlie and Algernon are two characters in this story.

———

1. Charles Schultz.
2. *Flowers for Algernon.*

ABOUT BOOKS

1. Who was Slue-Foot Sue?
2. *Tuned Out, Shadow of a Bull,* and *Hollywood Kid* are three of her books.

———

1. Pecos Bill's girlfriend.
2. Maia Wojciechowska.

ABOUT BOOKS

1. Who was Davy Crockett?
2. She wrote about lions in *Born Free* and *Forever Free.*

———

1. A frontiersman.
2. Joy Adamson.

ABOUT BOOKS

1. *20,000 Leagues Under the Sea* and *Journey to the Center of the Earth* are two books written by this author.
2. From the book *It's Like This, Cat,* where did Dave Mitchell live?

———

1. Jules Verne.
2. New York City.

ABOUT BOOKS

ABOUT BOOKS
1. This author wrote *The Hobbit* and *Lord of the Rings*.
2. Cherry, Dally, Johnny, and Pony Boy are characters in this book.

————

1. J.R.R. Tolkien.
2. *The Outsiders*.

ABOUT BOOKS
1. *A Christmas Carol* and *Oliver Twist* are two of his most famous books.
2. What was the name of the teacher in the book *Mitch and Amy* by Beverly Cleary?

————

1. Charles Dickens.
2. Miss Colby.

ABOUT BOOKS
1. This writer is the creator of Silver Chief.
2. *House of Secrets, The Witch's Daughter,* and *Three on the Run* are three of her books.

————

1. Jack O'Brien.
2. Nina Bawden.

ABOUT BOOKS
1. What was Stormalong's occupation?
2. This author wrote a story about an Indian girl who lived alone on an island for 18 years.

————

1. Sailor.
2. Scott O'Dell.

ABOUT BOOKS
1. In the "Encyclopedia Brown" books, what is Encyclopedia Brown's real name?
2. Cool, Fat Cat, Little Pie, and Buddy Williams are characters in this story.

————

1. Leroy Brown.
2. *Mystery of the Fat Cat.*

ABOUT BOOKS
1. Charlotte, Fern, Wilbur, and Mr. Arable are characters in this book.
2. *Mystery on Safari, Angel on Skis,* and *Love, Laurie* are three of her books.

————

1. *Charlotte's Web.*
2. Betty Cavanna.

ABOUT BOOKS

ABOUT BOOKS
1. Walter Farley is noted for writing many stories about this animal.
2. Nate Twitchell is the main character in this book.

———

1. Horse.
2. *The Enormous Egg.*

ABOUT BOOKS
1. She spoke with an echo in the book *A Wrinkle in Time.*
2. Who was Poseidon in Greek legends?

———

1. Mrs. Which.
2. God of the sea.

ABOUT BOOKS
1. Name Paul Bunyan's blue ox.
2. What happened to Medusa's hair in the Greek legend?

———

1. Babe.
2. Her hair turned to snakes.

ABOUT BOOKS
1. How does Dribble the turtle die in the book *Tales of a Fourth Grade Nothing*?
2. Byron, Mark, Cathy, and M & M are characters in this book.

———

1. Fudge swallowed him.
2. *That Was Then, This Is Now.*

ABOUT BOOKS
1 Willie Wonka, Grandpa Joe, Oompas, and Charlie are characters in this book.
2. *Edgar Allen, Lisa Bright and Dark,* and *Twink* are three stories written by this author.

———

1. *Charlie and the Chocolate Factory.*
2. John Newfeld.

ABOUT BOOKS
1. When Clara Barton grew up what did she become?
2. What was Annie Oakley's real name?

———

1. A nurse.
2. Annie Moses.

AUTHORS

AUTHORS
1. Who wrote *Black Stallion Returns*?
2. Who is the author of *Bridge to Terabithia*?

---

1. Walter Farley.
2. Katherine Paterson.

AUTHORS
1. Who wrote *Stallions of Lipizza*?
2. Who is the author of *Lassie Come-Home*?

---

1. Marguerite Henry.
2. Eric Knight.

AUTHORS
1. Who wrote *Bully of Barkham Street*?
2. Who is the author of *Sister of the Bride*?

---

1. Mary S. Stolz.
2. Beverly Cleary.

AUTHORS
1. Who wrote *It's Not the End of the World*?
2. Who is the author of *Tales of Olga Da Polga*?

---

1. Judy Blume.
2. Michael Bond.

AUTHORS
1. Who wrote *Henry Huggins*?
2. Who is the author of *Is That You, Miss Blue?*

---

1. Beverly Cleary.
2. M.E. Kerr.

AUTHORS
1. Who wrote *Me and Fat Glenda*?
2. Who is the author of *Kidnapped*?

---

1. Lila Perl.
2. Robert Louis Stevenson.

AUTHORS

AUTHORS
1. Who wrote *From Anna*?
2. Who is the author of *Getting Something on Maggie Marmelstein*?

———

1. Jean Little.
2. Marjorie W. Sharmat.

AUTHORS
1. Who wrote *Jacob Have I Loved*?
2. Who is the author of *James and the Giant Peach*?

———

1. Katherine Paterson.
2. Roald Dahl.

AUTHORS
1. Who wrote *Soup*?
2. Who is the author of *Charlie and the Chocolate Factory*?

———

1. Robert Newton Peck.
2. Roald Dahl.

AUTHORS
1. Who wrote *The Black Stallion*?
2. Who is the author of *Twenty-one Balloons*?

———

1. Walter Farley.
2. William Pene DuBois.

AUTHORS
1. Who wrote *Freckle Juice*?
2. Who is the author of *Dominic*?

———

1. Judy Blume.
2. William Steig.

AUTHORS
1. Who wrote *Old Yeller*?
2. Who is the author of *Julie of the Wolves*?

———

1. Fred Gipson.
2. Jean Craighead George.

AUTHORS

AUTHORS

1. Who wrote *Encyclopedia Brown Saves the Day?*
2. Who is the author of *Call of the Wild?*

———

1. Donald J. Sobol.
2. Jack London.

AUTHORS

1. Who wrote *Pippi Longstocking?*
2. Who is the author of *That Was Then, This Is Now?*

———

1. Astrid Lindgren.
2. S.E. Hinton.

AUTHORS

1. Who wrote *Starring Sally J. Freedman As Herself?*
2. Who is the author of *Durango Street?*

———

1. Judy Blume.
2. Frank Bonham.

AUTHORS

1. Who wrote *Socks?*
2. Who is the author of *Confessions of an Only Child?*

———

1. Beverly Cleary.
2. Norman Klein.

AUTHORS

1. Who wrote *Pistachio Prescription?*
2. Who is the author of *Black Beauty?*

———

1. Paula Danziger.
2. Anna Sewell.

AUTHORS

1. Who wrote *Me and the Terrible Two?*
2. Who is the author of *Bad Times of Irma Baumlein?*

———

1. Ellen Conford.
2. Carol Brink.

AUTHORS

AUTHORS
1. Who wrote *Tales of a Fourth Grade Nothing*?
2. Who is the author of *Robinson Crusoe*?

———

1. Judy Blume.
2. Daniel Defoe.

AUTHORS
1. Who wrote *Dinky Hocker Shoots Smack*?
2. Who is the author of *Escape to Witch Mountain*?

———

1. M.E. Kerr.
2. Alexander Key.

AUTHORS
1. Who wrote *The Cat Ate My Gymsuit*?
2. Who is the author of *Harriet, the Spy*?

———

1. Paula Danziger.
2. Louise Fitzhugh.

AUTHORS
1. Who wrote *Blubber*?
2. Who is the author of *Little Women*?

———

1. Judy Blume.
2. Louisa May Alcott.

AUTHORS
1. Who wrote *Philip Hall Likes Me*?
2. Who is the author of *Call It Courage*?

———

1. Betty Greene.
2. Armstrong Sperry.

AUTHORS
1. Who wrote *Trouble River*?
2. Who is the author of *Incredible Journey*?

———

1. Betsy Byars.
2. Sheila Burnford.

AUTHORS

AUTHORS
1. Who wrote *Tiger Eyes*?
2. Who is the author of *Anne of Green Gables*?

———

1. Judy Blume.
2. L.M. Montgomery.

AUTHORS
1. Who wrote *Summer of the Swans*?
2. Who is the author of *The Enormous Egg*?

———

1. Betsy Byars.
2. Oliver Butterworth.

AUTHORS
1. Who wrote *Gentlehands*?
2. Who is the author of *From the Mixed-up Files of Mrs. Basil E. Frankweiler*?

———

1. M.E. Kerr.
2. E.L. Konigsburg.

AUTHORS
1. Who wrote *Mouse and the Motorcycle*?
2. Who is the author of *Charlotte's Web*?

———

1. Beverly Cleary.
2. E.B. White.

AUTHORS
1. Who wrote *King of the Wind*?
2. Who is the author of *Anne of the Island*?

———

1. Marguerite Henry.
2. L.M. Montgomery.

AUTHORS
1. Who wrote *Iggie's House*?
2. Who is the author of *The High King*?

———

1. Judy Blume.
2. Lloyd Alexander.

AUTHORS

AUTHORS

1. Who wrote *Misty of Chincoteague*?
2. Who is the author of *Wind in the Willows*?

_____

1. Marguerite Henry.
2. Kenneth Grahame.

AUTHORS

1. Who wrote *A Bear Called Paddington*?
2. Who is the author of *Then Again, Maybe I Won't*?

_____

1. Michael Bond.
2. Judy Blume.

AUTHORS

1. Who wrote *Henry and Risby*?
2. Who is the author of *Honestly, Katie John*?

_____

1. Beverly Cleary.
2. Mary Calhoun.

AUTHORS

1. Who wrote *Mishmash*?
2. Who is the author of *Alice in Wonderland*?

_____

1. Molly Cone.
2. Lewis Carroll.

AUTHORS

1. Who wrote *Black Gold*?
2. Who is the author of *This Can't Be Happening at MacDonald Hall*?

_____

1. Marguerite Henry.
2. Gordon Korman.

AUTHORS

1. Who wrote *Ramona, the Pest*?
2. Who is the author of *Rumble Fish*?

_____

1. Beverly Cleary.
2. S.E. Hinton.

AUTHORS

AUTHORS
1. Who wrote *Stormy, Misty's Foal*?
2. Who is the author of . . . *And Now Miguel*?

————

1. Marguerite Henry.
2. Joseph Krumgold.

AUTHORS
1. Who wrote *The Hobbit*?
2. Who is the author of *Trumpet of the Swan*?

————

1. J.R.R. Tolkien.
2. E.B. White.

AUTHORS
1. Who wrote *Deenie*?
2. Who is the author of *Wolves of Willoughby Chase*?

————

1. Judy Blume.
2. Joan Aiken.

AUTHORS
1. Who wrote *Freaky Friday*?
2. Who is the author of *Witch of Blackbird Pond*?

————

1. Mary Rodgers.
2. Elizabeth George Speare.

AUTHORS
1. Who wrote *Confessions of a Teenage Baboon*?
2. Who is the author of *Mary Poppins*?

————

1. Paul Zindel.
2. Pamela L. Travers.

AUTHORS
1. Who wrote *Are You There God? It's Me, Margaret.*
2. Who is the author of *Lost in the Barrens*?

————

1. Judy Blume.
2. Farley Mowat.

AUTHORS

AUTHORS
1. Who wrote *The Pinballs*?
2. Who is the author of *Cat Who Went to Heaven*?

————

1. Betsy Byars.
2. Elizabeth Coatsworth.

AUTHORS
1. Who wrote *Island of the Blue Dolphins*?
2. Who is the author of *Treasure Island*?

————

1. Scott O'Dell.
2. Robert Louis Stevenson.

AUTHORS
1. Who wrote *Superfudge*?
2. Who is the author of *Gulliver's Travels*?

————

1. Judy Blume.
2. Jonathan Swift.

AUTHORS
1. Who wrote *Little House on the Prairie*?
2. Who is the author of *Incident at Hawk's Hill*?

————

1. Laura I. Wilder.
2. Allan W. Eckert.

AUTHORS
1. Who wrote *Encyclopedia Brown, Boy Detective*?
2. Who is the author of *Best Christmas Pageant Ever*?

————

1. Donald J. Sobol.
2. Barbara Robinson.

AUTHORS
1. Who wrote *Bats in Bunk Five*?
2. Who is the author of *Blue Willow*?

————

1. Paula Danziger.
2. Doris Gates.

DEWEY DECIMAL

DEWEY DECIMAL

1. What subject of books is represented by the number 595.7?
2. What do we call the division under the Dewey Decimal System where man writes about people and events that have occurred all over the world?

———

1. Insects.
2. History, Geography, and Biography.

DEWEY DECIMAL

1. What class division would you check to locate a book on Switzerland?
2. Books on squids, octopuses, and devilfish have this call number.

———

1. 900.
2. 594.

DEWEY DECIMAL

1. What class division would you check to locate a book on pioneers?
2. Books about electricity have this call number.

———

1. 900.
2. 537.

DEWEY DECIMAL

1. What class division would you check to get information on drag racing?
2. What do we call the division under the Dewey Decimal System that deals with man trying to understand all things in nature?

———

1. 700.
2. Science or Pure Science.

DEWEY DECIMAL

1. What class division would you check if you wanted information on monkeys?
2. Books on this pet have the call number 636.7.

———

1. 500.
2. Dogs.

DEWEY DECIMAL

1. What class division would you check to locate a book on deserts?
2. Books on microbes have this call number.

———

1. 500 or 900.
2. 576.

DEWEY DECIMAL

DEWEY DECIMAL
1. What class division would you check to locate a book on drawing?
2. Books about fishing, hunting, and shooting have this call number.

————

1. 700.
2. 799.

DEWEY DECIMAL
1. What class division would you check to locate a book on the French language?
2. What kind of ball would you use for the sport with the call number 796.352?

————

1. 400.
2. Golf ball.

DEWEY DECIMAL
1. What class division would you check to locate a book on music?
2. Name the country represented by the call number 914.94.

————

1. 700.
2. Switzerland.

DEWEY DECIMAL
1. Name the continent represented by the call number 915.
2. Books on this pet have the call number 636.1.

————

1. Asia.
2. Horses.

DEWEY DECIMAL
1. What subject of books is represented by the call number 395?
2. Name the country represented by the number 914.4.

————

1. Manners or etiquette.
2. France.

DEWEY DECIMAL
1. What subject is represented by the call number 821?
2. Name the country represented by the call number 917.3.

————

1. Poetry.
2. United States.

DEWEY DECIMAL

DEWEY DECIMAL

1. What class division would you check to locate a book about safety?
2. What is the most important thing to remember about the Dewey Decimal System of Classification

———

1. 600.
2. All books on the same topic are grouped together on the shelves because they have the same call number.

DEWEY DECIMAL

1. What class division would you check to locate a book about Helen Keller?
2. What would you find funny in books with the call number 793.7?

———

1. 900.
2. Riddles and jokes.

DEWEY DECIMAL

1. What class division would you check to locate a book on the Aztecs?
2. What do we call the division under the Dewey Decimal System where man takes time to enjoy his leisure time?

———

1. 900.
2. Fine Arts, Recreation, or Fine Arts and Recreation.

DEWEY DECIMAL

1. Books on this pet have the call number 636.8.
2. Name the country represented by the call number 914.5.

———

1. Cats.
2. Italy.

DEWEY DECIMAL

1. Give the call number for collective biography.
2. Books about worms, lobsters, and crabs have this call number.

———

1. 920.
2. 595.

DEWEY DECIMAL

1. What class division would you check to locate books on metals?
2. What do we call the division under the Dewey Decimal System that deals with man writing poetry?

———

1. 600.
2. Literature.

DEWEY DECIMAL

DEWEY DECIMAL

1. Who is the Dewey Decimal System of Classification named after?
2. What do we call the division under the Dewey Decimal System that deals with how man thinks?

---

1. Melvil Dewey.
2. Philosophy and Psychology.

DEWEY DECIMAL

1. What class division would you check to locate a picture of poison ivy?
2. What kind of ball would you use for the sport with the call number 794.6?

---

1. 500.
2. Bowling.

DEWEY DECIMAL

1. What class division would you check to locate a book on gymnastics?
2. Name the country represented by the call number 918.1.

---

1. 700.
2. Brazil.

DEWEY DECIMAL

1. Name the continent represented by the call number 914?
2. This call number represents books about the Vikings.

---

1. Europe.
2. 948.

DEWEY DECIMAL

1. What subject of books is represented by the call number 641.5?
2. Why are the people written about in the 910.92s famous?

---

1. Cookbooks.
2. They were explorers.

DEWEY DECIMAL

1. What subject of books is represented by the call number 398.2?
2. Name the country represented by the call number 917.1.

---

1. Folk lore, fairy tales, or tall tales.
2. Canada.

DEWEY DECIMAL

DEWEY DECIMAL
1. What subject of books is represented by the call number 520?
2. Name the country represented by the call number 917.2.

_____

1. Astronomy.
2. Mexico.

DEWEY DECIMAL
1. What class division would you check to find information about insects?
2. What kind of ball would you use for the sport with the call number 796.357?

_____

1. 500.
2. Baseball.

DEWEY DECIMAL
1. What subject of books is represented by the call number 598?
2. What do we call the division under the Dewey Decimal System where man applies his knowledge about nature and makes useful things?

_____

1. Birds.
2. Applied Science, Useful Arts, or Technology.

DEWEY DECIMAL
1. Name the continent represented by the call number 916.
2. Books about trees have this call number.

_____

1. Africa.
2. 582.

DEWEY DECIMAL
1. What class division would you check to locate a book on manners?
2. Books about weeds and wildflowers have this call number.

_____

1. 300.
2. 581.

DEWEY DECIMAL
1. What class division would you check to locate a book on chess?
2. Name the country represented by the call number 915.2.

_____

1. 700.
2. Japan.

DEWEY DECIMAL

DEWEY DECIMAL

1. What class division would you check to locate a Bible story to read?
2. Name the country represented by the call number 914.92.

_____

1. 200.
2. Holland.

DEWEY DECIMAL

1. What class division would you check to locate a book on occupations?
2. Name the country represented by the call number 914.1

_____

1. 300.
2. Scotland.

DEWEY DECIMAL

1. Name the continent represented by the call number 917.
2. What do we call the division under the Dewey Decimal System that deals with man communicating with his neighbors?

_____

1. North America.
2. Language or Philology.

DEWEY DECIMAL

1. What kind of stories are represented by the number 398.8?
2. Books about space are represented by this number.

_____

1. Nursery rhymes or Mother Goose rhymes.
2. 629.4.

DEWEY DECIMAL

1. What subject of books is represented by the number 598.1?
2. Books about spiders have this call number.

_____

1. Snakes, lizards, turtles, or alligators.
2. 595.4.

DEWEY DECIMAL

1. What kind of stories are represented by the number 920 or 921?
2. Name the country represented by the call number 915.1.

_____

1. Biography or stories about famous people.
2. China.

DEWEY DECIMAL

DEWEY DECIMAL

1. The call number 560 or 568 represents this animal, which roamed the earth years ago.
2. What do we call the division under the Dewey Decimal System where man thinks about his neighbors?

_____

1. Dinosaurs.
2. Sociology or Social Sciences.

DEWEY DECIMAL

1. What class division would you check to locate a Christmas story?
2. What kind of ball would you use for the sport with the call number 796.33?

_____

1. 300.
2. Soccer ball or football.

DEWEY DECIMAL

1. What class division would you check to locate a book about Christopher Columbus?
2. Books about rocks and minerals have this call number.

_____

1. 900.
2. 552.

DEWEY DECIMAL

1. These native people, found in the 970.1s, were warriors of long ago.
2. What country is represented by the call number 919.4.

_____

1. Indians.
2. Australia.

DEWEY DECIMAL

1. What class division would you check to locate a book on weather?
2. Books about magnets have this call number.

_____

1. 500.
2. 538.

DEWEY DECIMAL

1. What subject of books is represented by the number 591?
2. Books about fish have this call number.

_____

1. Animals.
2. 597.

DEWEY DECIMAL

DEWEY DECIMAL

1. These native people found in the 919.8s used kayaks while fishing.
2. What do we call the division under the Dewey Decimal System that deals with how man sees his God?

———

1. Eskimo or Inuit.
2. Religion.

DEWEY DECIMAL

1. Name the continent represented by the call number 918.
2. Books on codes and secret writing have this call number.

———

1. South America.
2. 652.

DEWEY DECIMAL

1. What class division would you check to locate a book on airplanes?
2. Name the country represented by the call number 914.2.

———

1. 300 or 600.
2. Great Britain.

DEWEY DECIMAL

1. What class division would you check to locate information on architecture?
2. What do we call the division under the Dewey Decimal System where books such as encyclopedias and other reference books are kept?

———

1. 700.
2. General Works.

DEWEY DECIMAL

1. What class division would you check to locate a book that contained a recipe for chocolate chip cookies?
2. What kind of ball would you use for the sport with the call number 796.32?

———

1. 600.
2. Basketball, volleyball, or net ball.

DEWEY DECIMAL

1. What class division would you check to locate a book on hobbies?
2. What hobby would you be involved in if you took out books from the 770s to assist you?

———

1. 700.
2. Photography.

LIBRARY TRIVIA

LIBRARY TRIVIA

1. What is the part of a book that usually shows on a library shelf?
2. What do we call the city in which a publisher is located?

———

1. Spine.
2. Place of publication.

LIBRARY TRIVIA

1. What names do we give to stories such as *Hercules*, *Zeus*, and *Prometheus*?
2. What does ABC order mean?

———

1. Myths or mythology.
2. Alphabetical order.

LIBRARY TRIVIA

1. Easy to read books use what letter to identify them?
2. What is the explanation of a word called?

———

1. E.
2. Meaning or definition.

LIBRARY TRIVIA

1. If you wish to know the title of a book written by Jean Little, what letter of the alphabet would you look under?
2. What reference book would give us voting statistics for the previous year?

———

1. L.
2. World almanac.

LIBRARY TRIVIA

1. What kind of book is *Pecos Bill*?
2. What name is given to the page that contains additional facts about information in the book?

———

1. A tall tale or legend.
2. An appendix.

LIBRARY TRIVIA

1. What name do we give stories such as *The Tortoise and the Hare* and *The Fox and the Grapes*?
2. Webster's *Geographical Dictionary* is an example of what kind of a book?

———

1. Fables.
2. A gazetteer.

LIBRARY TRIVIA

LIBRARY TRIVIA

1. What do we call the pocket to hold a borrower's card?
2. What name is given to the extra pages at the front and back of a book that is usually left blank?

   _____

1. Book pocket.
2. Endpapers.

LIBRARY TRIVIA

1. What do we call the card used to sign out books?
2. What do we call a section of a book that usually has a heading or number at the beginning?

   _____

1. Borrower's card.
2. Chapter.

LIBRARY TRIVIA

1. What part of the author's name is most important for library usage?
2. What reference book would be most useful if you wished a factual description of a country?

   _____

1. Last name.
2. Encyclopedia.

LIBRARY TRIVIA

1. What is the best reference book to use when looking up information on persons and places?
2. When the top line of a catalog card is printed entirely in capital letters what does it indicate?

   _____

1. An encyclopedia.
2. A subject card.

LIBRARY TRIVIA

1. What name is given to the page in a book that contains a short note from the author in which a special person is remembered?
2. If you wished to look up some bare facts and statistics about a country, what would be the best reference book to use?

   _____

1. Dedication page.
2. World almanac.

LIBRARY TRIVIA

1. What do we call a group of books that gives information on a variety of topics?
2. What name is given to the names of some articles printed in bold type and listed in the index of an encyclopedia?

   _____

1. Encyclopedia.
2. Main entry.

LIBRARY TRIVIA

LIBRARY TRIVIA

1. What is the method for arranging nonfiction books in order called?
2. What was Randolph Caldecott's occupation?

———

1. Dewey Decimal Classification System or Library of Congress.
2. Illustrator of childrens' books.

LIBRARY TRIVIA

1. If you wanted to locate cities, states, or rivers what reference book would you use?
2. What illustration is shown on the reverse side of the Caldecott Medal?

———

1. An atlas.
2. "Four and twenty blackbirds baked in a pie."

LIBRARY TRIVIA

1. If you wished to know the title of a book written by Farley Mowat what letter of the alphabet would you look under in the card catalog?
2. This part of a book lists subjects in alphabetical order and gives the pages where they can be found?

———

1. M.
2. An index.

LIBRARY TRIVIA

1. What letter of the alphabet would you look under in the card catalog to locate *The Christmas Kitten*?
2. If a library has more than one book by the same author in the fiction section how are they arranged on the shelf?

———

1. C.
2. Alphabetically by their titles.

LIBRARY TRIVIA

1. What reference book would be most useful if you wanted to locate pictures of the presidents of the United States?
2. What illustration is shown on the face of the Caldecott Medal?

———

1. Encyclopedia.
2. "John Gilpin's ride."

LIBRARY TRIVIA

1. If you want to find the correct usage of a word, what is the best reference book to use?
2. What name do we give to the file drawers that hold clippings?

———

1. A dictionary.
2. Vertical file.

LIBRARY TRIVIA

LIBRARY TRIVIA

1. Into how many main groups is the nonfiction section of the library divided?
2. What do we call a list of material the author referred to when writing the book?

_____

1. 10.
2. A bibliography.

LIBRARY TRIVIA

1. By what other name is the *Readers' Guide to Periodical Literature* known?
2. This is a book for small children that contains many illustrations.

_____

1. *Reader's Guide.*
2. Picture book.

LIBRARY TRIVIA

1. What letter of the alphabet would you look under in the card catalog to locate *The Sea Islanders*?
2. This is found in some books and explains the difficult words found in that book.

_____

1. S.
2. A glossary.

LIBRARY TRIVIA

1. What name do we give to books such as *The Three Billy Goats Gruff, Snow White*, and *Rapunzel*?
2. What do we call one book in a group of books?

_____

1. Fairy tale or folk tale.
2. Volume.

LIBRARY TRIVIA

1. If you wished to know the capital of your state or province, what would be the best reference book to use?
2. This book lists the names of important people in alphabetical order and gives some important facts about each person.

_____

1. An atlas.
2. A biographical dictionary.

LIBRARY TRIVIA

1. If you are writing a report and need information from different sources, where would you look first to find out what materials are in your library?
2. What do we call information printed in nonfiction books or encylopedias?

_____

1. Card catalog.
2. Facts.

LIBRARY TRIVIA

LIBRARY TRIVIA
1. What do we call a person who has written a book?
2. What year was the first Caldecott Medal awarded?

_____

1. Author.
2. 1938.

LIBRARY TRIVIA
1. What should you use to keep your place in a book when you are not reading it?
2. What information can be found on the back (verso) side of a title page in a book?

_____

1. A bookmark.
2. Copyright date.

LIBRARY TRIVIA
1. What do we call a person who has drawn pictures for a book?
2. When you look at a catalog card, what tells you where a book is located in the library?

_____

1. Illustrator.
2. Call number of the book.

LIBRARY TRIVIA
1. What letter on the call label of a book tells you that a book is a reference book?
2. What kind of book will give us up-to-date information on world events?

_____

1. R.
2. Almanac.

LIBRARY TRIVIA
1. If a friend wrote the true story of your life what would it be?
2. Give a definition of a gazetteer.

_____

1. Biography (individual).
2. A dictionary or index of geographical names.

LIBRARY TRIVIA
1. What do we call the part of a book that lists the chapters in the book?
2. If you wrote the true story of your own life what kind of book would it be?

_____

1. Table of contents.
2. An autobiography.

LIBRARY TRIVIA

LIBRARY TRIVIA

1. What do we call the edge of a book that is held together with stitches and glue?
2. To what is *The Abridged Readers' Guide to Periodical Literature* an index?

———

1. The spine.
2. Magazine articles.

LIBRARY TRIVIA

1. What is another name given to a periodical?
2. What name is given to the first and last words found at the top of the page in a dictionary?

———

1. Magazine.
2. Guide word.

LIBRARY TRIVIA

1. What is the best reference book to use when looking up information on events and ideas?
2. If you wish to locate political boundaries for certain countries, what is the best reference book to use?

———

1. An encyclopedia.
2. An atlas.

LIBRARY TRIVIA

1. How are the cards in the card catalog filed?
2. This is sometimes called a foreword and often tells what the book is about or why the author wrote it.

———

1. In alphabetical order.
2. Preface.

LIBRARY TRIVIA

1. What name do we give the person who keeps everything organized in the library?
2. This word is the most important word in the question and is always a person, place, or thing.

———

1. Librarian or resource person.
2. Key word.

LIBRARY TRIVIA

1. What name is given to books such as *Cinderella*, *The Three Bears*, and *Jack and the Beanstalk*?
2. What is a good reference book to use when writing a report?

———

1. Fairy tale or folk tale.
2. An encyclopedia.

LIBRARY TRIVIA

LIBRARY TRIVIA

1. What is a book with made-up stories in it called?
2. Where is the index in the *World Almanac*?

———

1. A fiction book.
2. In the front of the book.

LIBRARY TRIVIA

1. What protects the pages of a book?
2. What does the engraving on the Caldecott Medal say?

———

1. A cover.
2. For the most distinguished American picture book for children.

LIBRARY TRIVIA

1. What do we call a book that gives meanings of words in alphabetical order?
2. What do we call a book that has hundreds or thousands of short articles about the lives of famous people living or dead?

———

1. A dictionary.
2. A biographical dictionary.

LIBRARY TRIVIA

1. What are the stories about Paul Bunyan and Pecos Bill called?
2. What do we call a book of synonyms and antonyms classified according to ideas?

———

1. Tall tales or legends.
2. A thesaurus.

LIBRARY TRIVIA

1. What are books that contain true facts called?
2. After whom is the Caldecott Award named?

———

1. Nonfiction books.
2. Randolph Caldecott.

LIBRARY TRIVIA

1. Give me another word that means the same as illustrator.
2. If you wrote a book telling about the true life stories of several people you knew, what kind of book would it be?

———

1. Artist.
2. A collective biography.

LIBRARY TRIVIA

LIBRARY TRIVIA

1. What letter in the library represents fiction books?
2. What part of the atlas would you look at first when trying to find the location of a city?

_____

1. F.
2. Index.

LIBRARY TRIVIA

1. What letter of the alphabet in the card catalog would you look under to find the book with the title *The Enormous Egg*?
2. What are the three main kinds of cards in the card catalog?

_____

1. E.
2. Author, Subject, and Title.

LIBRARY TRIVIA

1. What is the main part of a book called?
2. What do we call the drawers that hold cards about every book in the library?

_____

1. Text, body, or story.
2. Card catalog.

LIBRARY TRIVIA

1. What do we call the part of a book that gives the title, author, illustrator, and publisher?
2. What are two kinds of cross reference cards?

_____

1. Title page.
2. "See" and "see also."

LIBRARY TRIVIA

1. What do we call a person or company who gets a writer's book sold to the public?
2. What is the desk where we sign out books in a library called?

_____

1. Publisher.
2. Circulation desk or charging desk.

LIBRARY TRIVIA

1. What is a book of maps called?
2. What way or ways can information be looked up in the *Abridged Readers' Guide to Periodical Literature*?

_____

1. An atlas.
2. By author and subject only.

NEWBERY AWARDS

NEWBERY AWARDS

1. Agba, Sham, Benjamin Biggle, and Jethro Coke are characters in this Newbery Award winner.
2. Who wrote *The Hero and the Crown*, a 1958 Newbery Award winner?

———

1. Henry, Marguerite, *King of the Wind.*
2. Robin McKinley

NEWBERY AWARDS

1. In which story did the artist not regret that he might suffer for Good Fortune's great moment of happiness?
2. Name the book by Joseph Krumgold that won the Newbery Award in 1954.

———

1. Coatsworth, Elizabeth, *The Cat Who Went to Heaven.*
2. *. . . And Now, Miguel.*

NEWBERY AWARDS

1. Why does an author receive a Newbery Award?
2. After whom was the Newbery Award named?

———

1. For the best children's book written in American literature in a particular year.
2. John Newbery.

NEWBERY AWARDS

1. From the book *Mrs. Frisby and the Rats of NIMH* by Robert C. O'Brien, what did NIMH stand for?
2. Name the book by Marguerite DeAngeli that won the Newbery Award in 1950.

———

1. National Institute of Mental Health
2. *The Door in the Wall.*

NEWBERY AWARDS

1. Name the two children who took up permanent residence at the Metropolitan Museum Art in the book *From the Mixed-up Files of Mrs. Basil E. Frankweiler.*
2. Who is the author of *The Grey King*?

———

1. Claudia and Jamie Kincaid.
2. Susan Cooper.

NEWBERY AWARDS

1. In what story did a poor black sharecropper steal for his hungry family, get sent to jail, and eventually return paralyzed and sick?
2. Who wrote *Rifles for Watie*?

———

1. Armstrong, William, *Sounder.*
2. Harold Keith.

NEWBERY AWARDS

NEWBERY AWARDS

1. In what story was a thirteen-year-old boy made to play his fife while kidnapped on a slave ship bound for Africa?
2. Name the book by Armstrong Sperry that won the Newbery Award in 1941.

———

1. Fox, Paula, *The Slave Dancer.*
2. *Call It Courage.*

NEWBERY AWARDS

1. In this book, the hero learned on the battlefield that his maimed hand could be cured so that he would be able to use a musket and eventually return to his trade as a silversmith.
2. Who wrote *Hitty, Her First Hundred Years*?

———

1. Forbes, Esther, *Johnny Tremain.*
2. Rachel Field.

NEWBERY AWARDS

1. Name the story in which Jeff Bussey, a Northerner, falls in love with a beautiful southern girl named Lucy Washbourne during Civil War times.
2. Who is the author of *Thimble Summer*, which won the Newbery Award in 1939.

———

1. Keith, Harold, *Rifles for Watie.*
2. Elizabeth Enright.

NEWBERY AWARDS

1. Birdie, Dovey, Shoestring Slater, and Miss Liddy are some of the characters found in this book.
2. Name the book by Henry William van Loon that won the first Newbery Award ever given.

———

1. Lenski, Lois, *Strawberry Girl.*
2. *The Story of Mankind.*

NEWBERY AWARDS

1. Ramo, Nanko, Karana, and a wild dog named Rontu are characters in this book.
2. Name the book by E.L. Konigsburg that won the Newbery Award in 1968.

———

1. O'Dell, Scott, *Island of the Blue Dolphins.*
2. *From the Mixed-up Files of Mrs. Basil E. Frankweiler.*

NEWBERY AWARDS

1. In this story, the Tillermans begin a new life with Gram in the Chesapeake Bay country that had once been their mamma's childhood home.
2. Name the book by Katherine Paterson that won the Newbery Award in 1978.

———

1. Voigt, Cynthia, *Dicey's Song.*
2. *Bridge to Terabithia.*

NEWBERY AWARDS

NEWBERY AWARDS

1. The thoughts and feelings of a young Navajo boy who wished to become a medicine man when he grew up are revealed in this story.
2. Name the book by Lloyd Alexander that won the 1969 Newbery Award.

———

1. Armer, Laura Adams, *Waterless Mountain.*
2. *The High King.*

NEWBERY AWARDS

1. Name the book that won the second Newbery Award in 1923.
2. Name the book by Jean Lee Latham that won the 1956 Newbery Award.

———

1. *The Voyages of Doctor Dolittle.*
2. *Carry on, Mr. Bowditch.*

NEWBERY AWARDS

1. In this story, Joseph is the hero of fifteenth century Poland.
2. Name the book by James Daugherty that won the Newbery Award in 1940.

———

1. Kelly, Eric P., *Trumpeter of Krakow.*
2. *Daniel Boone.*

NEWBERY AWARDS

1. In which story do we read about a girl who felt her younger sister Caroline had robbed her of all her hopes for schooling, her friends, her mother, and even her name?
2. Who wrote *Miracles on Maple Hill*, a 1957 Newbery Award winner?

———

1. Paterson, Katherine, *Jacob Have I Loved.*
2. Virginia Sorensen.

NEWBERY AWARDS

1. In this Newbery Award winner, a young Chinese boy became a coppersmith after a three-year apprenticeship.
2. Who wrote *Smoky, the Cowhorse*?

———

1. Lewis, Elizabeth Foreman, *Young Fu of the Upper Yangtze.*
2. Will James.

NEWBERY AWARDS

1. In the town of Serenity where Andy Rusch, Jr. lived, he had many friends but who became his special and very best friend?
2. Name the book by Susan Cooper that won the 1976 Newbery Award.

———

1. *Onion John*, by Joseph Krumgold.
2. *The Grey King.*

NEWBERY AWARDS

NEWBERY AWARDS

1. This story is about a boy's affection for a stray tomcat, his friendship with a troubled nineteen-year-old boy, and his first shy friendship with a girl named Mary.
2. Who wrote *Strawberry Girl*, a 1946 Newbery Award winner?

————

1. Neville, Emily, *It's Like This, Cat.*
2. Lois Lenski.

NEWBERY AWARDS

1. Professor William Waterman Sherman told about his brief stay on the island of Krakatoa in this Newbery Award winner.
2. Name the book written by Elizabeth Yates that became a 1951 Newbery Award winner.

————

1. Du Bois, William Pene, *The Twenty-one Balloons.*
2. *Amos Fortune, Free Man.*

NEWBERY AWARDS

1. In what story did a young Eskimo girl rebelling against her home situation become lost, without food or a compass, on the North Slope of Alaska?
2. Name the book by Ellen Raskin that won the Newbery Award in 1979.

————

1. George, Jean C., *Julie of the Wolves.*
2. *The Westing Game.*

NEWBERY AWARDS

1. Jerry, Rachel, Addie Egan, and Dick Badger are characters in this Newbery Award winner.
2. Who is the author of *Roll of Thunder, Hear My Cry*?

————

1. Estes, Eleanor, *Ginger Pye.*
2. Mildred D. Taylor.

NEWBERY AWARDS

1. This is the story of a Negro slave born in the seventeenth century who became an accomplished and respected artist in Spain through the efforts of his benefactor.
2. Who wrote *A Wrinkle in Time*?

————

1. De Trevino, Elizabeth B., *I, Juan de Pareja.*
2. Madeleine L'Engle.

NEWBERY AWARDS

1. This story describes a special friendship between a boy named Jess and a girl named Leslie and their new world of imagination and unexpected tragedy.
2. Name the book written by Cornelia Meigs that became the 1934 Newbery Award winner.

————

1. Paterson, Katherine, *Bridge to Terabithia.*
2. *Invincible Louisa.*

NEWBERY AWARDS

NEWBERY AWARDS

1. In what story did Charlie, a mentally retarded boy, have his watch removed from his arm by boys offering candy just so they could upset and tease him?

2. Who is the author of *Adam of the Road*, a 1943 Newbery Award winner?

———

1. Byars, Betsy, *Summer of the Swans*.
2. Elizabeth Janet Gray.

NEWBERY AWARDS

1. In which story did Julie Trelling grow from a tantrum-throwing seven-year-old to a gracious young woman of seventeen?

2. Name the book by Elizabeth Lewis that won the Newbery Award in 1933.

———

1. Hunt, Irene, *Up a Road Slowly*.
2. *Young Fu of the Upper Yangtze*.

NEWBERY AWARDS

1. Uncle Analdas, Little Georgie, Robin, and Porkey are characters in this Newbery Award winner.

2. Name the book by Maia Wojciechowska that won the 1965 Newbery Award.

———

1. Lawson, Robert, *Rabbit Hill*.
2. *Shadow of a Bull*.

NEWBERY AWARDS

1. In this story, six children overcame many obstacles to make a dream come true by eventually getting a stork on every roof in Shora.

2. Who wrote *Caddie Woodlawn*?

———

1. DeJong, Meindert, *The Wheel on the School*.
2. Carol R. Brink.

NEWBERY AWARDS

1. In what story did a young lame boy whose mother attended the Queen and whose father went off to war, get cared for by Brother Luke?

2. Name the book by Paula Fox that won the 1974 Newbery Award.

———

1. DeAngeli, Marguerite, *The Door in the Wall*.
2. *The Slave Dancer*.

NEWBERY AWARDS

1. From the book, *Witch of Blackbird Pond*, name the sixteen-year-old girl who was sent to live with her aunt, Mistress Wood, in Wethersfield.

2. Who is the author of *Dear Mr. Henshaw*?

———

1. Kit Tyler.
2. Beverly Cleary.

NEWBERY AWARDS

NEWBERY AWARDS

1. In this story, a boy had three things to comfort him, his harp, his friend Perkin, and his dog Nick, while his father was in France attending Minstrel's school.
2. Name the book by Irene Hunt that won the Newbery Award in 1967.

———

1. Gray, Elizabeth Janet, *Adam of the Road.*
2. *Up a Road Slowly.*

NEWBERY AWARDS

1. Name the boy whose father had been the greatest bull fighter in all of Spain and who was expected to follow in his father's footsteps even though he did not want to do so.
2. Name the book by Esther Forbes that won the 1944 Newbery Award.

———

1. Manola Olivar in *Shadow of a Bull.*
2. *Johnny Tremain.*

NEWBERY AWARDS

1. In this story, Polynesia, the parrot assisted in the writing of their many adventures.
2. Who is the author of *The Trumpeter of Krakow*?

———

1. Lofting, Hugh, *The Voyages of Doctor Dolittle.*
2. Eric P. Kelly.

NEWBERY AWARDS

1. In this story, this animal had been born with a natural fear and hate of all humans except a man named Clint, who first entered his life when he was about four years old.
2. Who is the author of *Rabbit Hill*?

———

1. James, Will, *Smoky, the Cowhorse.*
2. Robert Lawson.

NEWBERY AWARDS

1. In what story did a young boy, determined to conquer his fear of the sea, set off in a canoe, alone except for his little dog and pet albatross?
2. Name the book written by Elizabeth George Speare that won the 1959 Newbery Award.

———

1. Sperry, Armstrong, *Call It Courage.*
2. *The Witch of Blackbird Pond.*

NEWBERY AWARDS

1. This story took place during the time of King Charles and involved a young boy named Philip, a member of a pirate crew who awaited the hangman on his return to England.
2. Name the book by Meindert DeJong that won the Newbery Award in 1955.

———

1. Hawes, Charles Boardman, *The Dark Frigate.*
2. *The Wheel on the School.*

NEWBERY AWARDS

NEWBERY AWARDS

1. In what story did sixteen people get invited to the reading of a strange will belonging to a very rich man, each pair given $10,000 and a set of clues that could eventually make them millionaires?
2. Name the book by Katherine Paterson that won the Newbery Award in 1981.

———

1. Raskin, Ellen, *The Westing Game.*
2. *Jacob Have I Loved.*

NEWBERY AWARDS

1. This story, written by Lloyd Alexander, is the finale to the chronicles of Prydain.
2. Name the book by Elizabeth George Speare that won the Newbery Award in 1962.

———

1. *The High King.*
2. *The Bronze Bow.*

NEWBERY AWARDS

1. Daniel Bar Jamin wanted only to help drive the Roman legions from the land of Israel so he could revenge the death of his father and mother in this story.
2. Who wrote *The White Stag*, a 1938 Newbery Award winner?

———

1. Speare, Elizabeth George, *The Bronze Bow.*
2. Kate Seredy.

NEWBERY AWARDS

1. In which story did Garnet and Citronella own a tree house, go to town in Mr. Freebody's truck, and fatten up a pig named Timmy with cod liver oil and choice scraps?
2. Who wrote *Carry On, Mr. Bowditch*?

———

1. Enright, Elizabeth, *Thimble Summer.*
2. Jean Lee Latham.

NEWBERY AWARDS

1. In what year did *The Story of Mankind* by Hendrik William van Loon win the first Newbery Award?
2. Who wrote *Mrs. Frisby and the Rats of NIMH*?

———

1. 1922.
2. Robert C. O'Brien.

NEWBERY AWARDS

1. Name the story in which an African boy was captured at fifteen by slave traders, brought to Massachusetts where he was sold as a slave, and eventually set up his own tanning business in the small village of Jaffrey, New Hampshire.
2. Who wrote *M.C. Higgins the Great*?

———

1. Yates, Elizabeth, *Amos Fortune, Free Man.*
2. Virginia Hamilton.

NEWBERY AWARDS

NEWBERY AWARDS

1. In this story the main character held a secret wish in his heart and yearned to go with the men in his family to the Sangre de Cristo Mountains.
2. Who wrote *The Matchlock Gun*?

———

1. Krumgold, Joseph, . . . *And Now Miguel.*
2. Walter D. Edmonds.

NEWBERY AWARDS

1. Tom, Warren, Hetty, and Indian John were real people brought to life in a pioneer story that took place in the state of Wisconsin.
2. Who wrote *Young Fu of the Upper Yangtze*?

———

1. Brink, Carol R., *Caddie Woodlawn.*
2. Elizabeth Lewis.

NEWBERY AWARDS

1. In this story a boy sat up on a forty-foot pole dreaming of escape for himself and his family.
2. Name the book by Ruth Sawyer that won the Newbery Award in 1937.

———

1. Hamilton, Virginia, *M.C. Higgins, the Great.*
2. *Roller Skates.*

NEWBERY AWARDS

1. In what story did Cusi, an Indian boy, live with Chuto, an old llama herder, and his special pet Misti?
2. Name the book by Elizabeth Coatsworth that won the Newbery Award in 1931.

———

1. Clark, Ann Nolan, *Secret of the Andes.*
2. *The Cat Who Went to Heaven.*

NEWBERY AWARDS

1. Name the story in which a doll carved from a piece of white ash had many exciting adventures on land and sea.
2. Who is the author of *It's Like This, Cat*?

———

1. Field, Rachel, *Hitty, Her First Hundred Years.*
2. Emily Neville.

NEWBERY AWARDS

1. This story, set in Mississippi at the height of the Depression, describes a family's struggle and determination not to be beaten down because they were black.
2. Who is the author of *Onion John*, which won the Newbery Award in 1960?

———

1. Taylor, Mildred D., *Roll of Thunder, Hear My Cry.*
2. Joseph Krumgold.

SUPER DOOBY
PLAYERS' SCORES

PLAYERS	ABOUT BOOKS	AUTHORS	DEWEY DECIMAL	LIBRARY TRIVIA	NEWBERY AWARDS	TOTAL SCORE

ALPHA DOOBY FICTION ACTIVITIES

Practice in Arranging Fiction Books in Order

ALPHA DOOBY FICTION ACTIVITIES

Game Objectives:

1. To familiarize students with the arrangement of fiction books on library shelves.
2. To reinforce the ideas that:
   a. Fiction books are arranged on the shelves in alphabetical order according to the author's last name.
   b. If more than one book is written by the same author, the books are arranged alphabetically according to the title.
   c. If there is more than one author with the same last name, the books are arranged alphabetically by the author's first name.
3. To make working with and learning about arranging fiction books in alphabetical order by authors' names and titles of books an interesting, stimulating, and enjoyable activity.

Uses:

- These Alpha Dooby fiction activities can be used as a class activity, with each student working on his or her own set. The activities can also be used with small groups of students working together.
- Alpha Dooby Fiction Activities can be used to train library club members in all aspects of shelving fiction books in correct alphabetical order.
- The activities can be used to introduce, reinforce, or culminate lessons taught on any aspect of alphabetical arrangement in library-related activities.
- The activities can be used in a library, a classroom, or any activity center.

Materials Needed:

- Scissors
- Copier machine
- 10 book card pockets, 10 folders, or 10 envelopes
- Marking pens
- *optional:* Clear self-stick vinyl
- *optional:* Tagboard
- *optional:* Glue

Construction Suggestions:

1. Make the number of copies of each set you need for the students, and write the numbers 1 through 10 or 1 through 15 on the backs of the book spines.
2. Cut out each book spine and let the students color and decorate them if desired. Keep each set in a book card pocket, folder, or envelope. (*Note:* For more durability, mount the spines on tagboard and then cover with clear self-stick vinyl. Remember to print the numbers on the spines before covering them with the vinyl and cutting out.)

3. Explain to the students the instructions for using each set of book spines. Write these instructions on the card pocket (or folder or envelope) for each set (see the sample in the illustration):

Set 1—Arrange Fiction books in alphabetical order by author's last name, A–Z (10 titles).

Set 2—Arrange Easy Fiction books in alphabetical order by author's last name, A–Z (10 titles).

Set 3—Arrange Fiction books in alphabetical order by author's last name, A–Z (15 titles).

Set 4—Author—Judy BLUME

Arrange Fiction books in order by title of book. Check second letter of first word in some titles (10 titles).

Set 5—Author—Elsa BIALK

Arrange Fiction books in order by title of book. Check second, third, or fourth word in titles (10 titles).

Set 6—Author—Donald J. SOBOL

Arrange Fiction books in order by title of book. Check third, fourth, fifth, sixth, seventh, or eighth word in titles (10 titles).

Set 7—Arrange Fiction books in order by second or third letter of author's last name. Check first name of authors named Smith. Check titles if there is more than one book by the same author (15 titles).

Set 8—Author—Dr. SEUSS

Arrange Easy Fiction books in alphabetical order by title of book. Check second or third word in title. Check second or third letter of first word in some titles (15 titles).

Set 9—Arrange Fiction books in order by third letter in author's last name. Check first name of authors named Haas, Hall, and Harris. Check titles if there is more than one book by same author (15 titles).

Set 10—Author—Beverly CLEARY

Arrange Fiction books in order by title of book. Check first, second, third, and fourth word in titles. Check second letter in first word of some titles (15 titles).

4. Make enough copies of the bookends so that students can color, laminate, and cut them out when using a set of book spines. The bookends can then be placed in the card pocket along with the spines.

Playing Suggestions:

1. Shuffle the book spines in each set so that they are not in the correct order.

2. Have the students arrange the spines in the order they feel is correct. Then ask them to turn each book spine over to check the answers. If the

spines have been arranged correctly, the numbers 1 through 10 or 1 through 15 will be in order. If not, let the students try to determine what is correct. Then shuffle the book spines and try again.

3. When the students are finished working with a set, make sure all book spines are returned to the proper folder, envelope, or card pocket.

4. Have students work with as many different sets as possible so that skills in all aspects of alphabetical arrangement of FICTION books will be learned or reinforced.

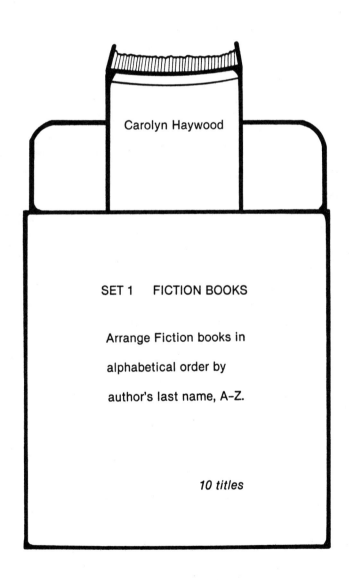

Carolyn Haywood

SET 1   FICTION BOOKS

Arrange Fiction books in

alphabetical order by

author's last name, A–Z.

10 titles

Setting Up Activity Centers:

1. Place at least *one* copy of each set in a small box for use in the center, and have each set in a card pocket, envelope, or folder. (You might want to have FICTION and NONFICTION sets in different boxes.)

2. Type or write the instructions on the front of each box, as shown in the sample illustration:

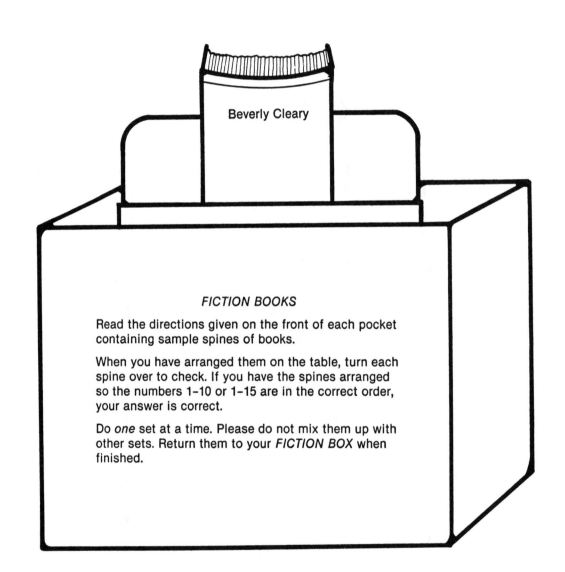

Beverly Cleary

FICTION BOOKS

Read the directions given on the front of each pocket containing sample spines of books.

When you have arranged them on the table, turn each spine over to check. If you have the spines arranged so the numbers 1–10 or 1–15 are in the correct order, your answer is correct.

Do *one* set at a time. Please do not mix them up with other sets. Return them to your *FICTION BOX* when finished.

General Rules for Arranging Fiction Books in Order:

1. Most fiction books are usually arranged on the shelves according to a *call letter*. The letter F may be used for fiction for older students. The letter E may be used for easy reading stories, and the letter X may be used to identify picture book stories.

2. All fiction books with the same call letter will then be arranged on the shelves in alphabetical order according to the author's *last* name. The book *Ramona the Pest* by Beverly Cleary, for example, would be placed in the Cs.

	Ramona the Pest	
F CAR	F CLE	F CRA

3. Sometimes books must be arranged in alphabetical order by the third and fourth letters of an author's last name. Thus, CLARKE would come before CLEARY.

4. When arranging fiction books written by the same author, you put them in order according to the title of the book. Remember that "A," "An," and "The" at the beginning of a title do not count. Thus, *The Mouse and the Motorcycle* by Beverly Cleary would come before *Ramona the Pest*.

5. Fiction books written by the same author with titles that start the same, such as "The Tizz" series, must be put in alphabetical order by looking at the third, fourth, fifth, or more words in the title. *Tizz on a Horse Farm*, for example, would come before *Tizz on a Trail Ride*.

6. Fiction books written by authors with the same last name have to be filed by using their first names. Thus, "Bond, Gladys" would come before "Bond, Michael."

ALPHA DOOBY
FICTION ACTIVITIES

Book Spine Sets

SET 1
ARRANGING FICTION BOOKS IN ORDER
BY AUTHOR'S LAST NAME, A-Z

Checklist of books used — 10 titles in set.

1.	F ALC	Alcott, Louisa M.	Little Women
2.	F BON	Bond, Michael	A Bear Called Paddington
3.	F FAR	Farley, Walter	The Black Stallion
4.	F GIP	Gipson, Fred	Old Yeller
5.	F HAY	Haywood, Carolyn	"C" Is for Cupcake
6.	F LEV	Levy, Elizabeth	Computer That Said Steal Me
7.	F MON	Montgomery, L.M.	Anne of Green Gables
8.	F PEL	Pellowski, Anne	Betsy's Up-and-Down Year
9.	F SUT	Sutton, Jane	Confessions of an Orange Octopus
10.	F WAR	Warner, Gertrude C.	The Yellow House Mystery

These fiction books are read by boys and girls age 8 to 14 years.

WEST BRIDGEWATER PUBLIC LIBRARY
80 Howard Street
West Bridgewater, MA 02379

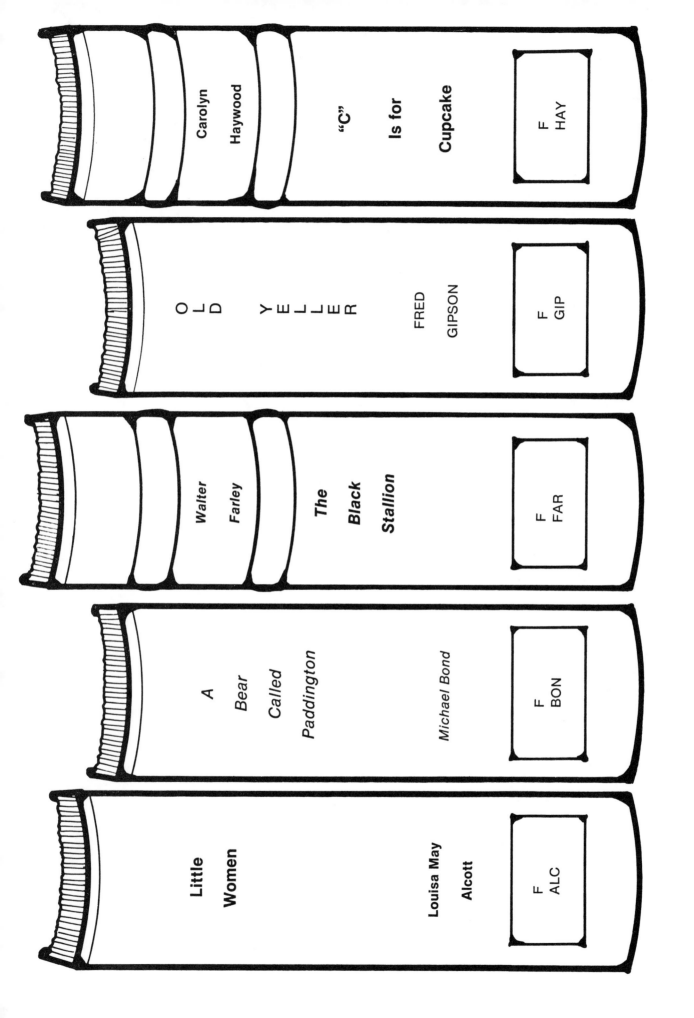

Answer Key

Starting from left to right, the correct order of these books is:

    Alcott—1
    Bond—2
    Farley—3
    Gipson—4
    Haywood—5

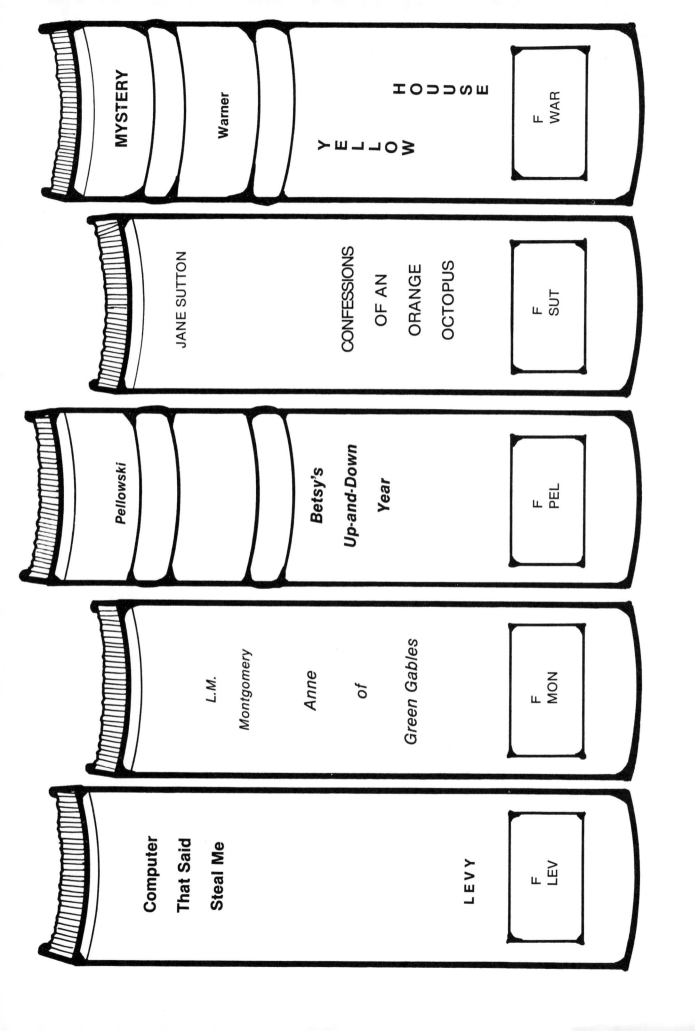

Answer Key

Starting from left to right, the correct order of these books is:

    Levy—6
    Montgomery—7
    Pellowski—8
    Sutton—9
    Warner—10

SET 2
ARRANGING EASY READING FICTION BOOKS IN ORDER BY AUTHOR'S LAST NAME, A-Z

Checklist of books used — 10 titles in set.

1.	E AND	Anderson, Clarence	Blaze and Thunderbolt
2.	E CAL	Calhoun, Mary	Wobble, the Witch Cat
3.	E FRE	Freeman, Don	Dandelion
4.	E JOH	Johnston, Tony	Happy Birthday, Mole and Troll
5.	E NIC	Nicki, Peter	Crocodile Crocodile
6.	E PAR	Parish, Peggy	Good Work, Amelia Bedelia
7.	E REY	Rey, H.A.	Curious George
8.	E THA	Thayer, Jane	Clever Raccoon
9.	E VIO	Viorst, Judith	Rosie and Michael
10.	E WIS	Wiseman, Bernard	Morris Goes to School

These easy reading books are read by boys and girls age 6 to 9 years.

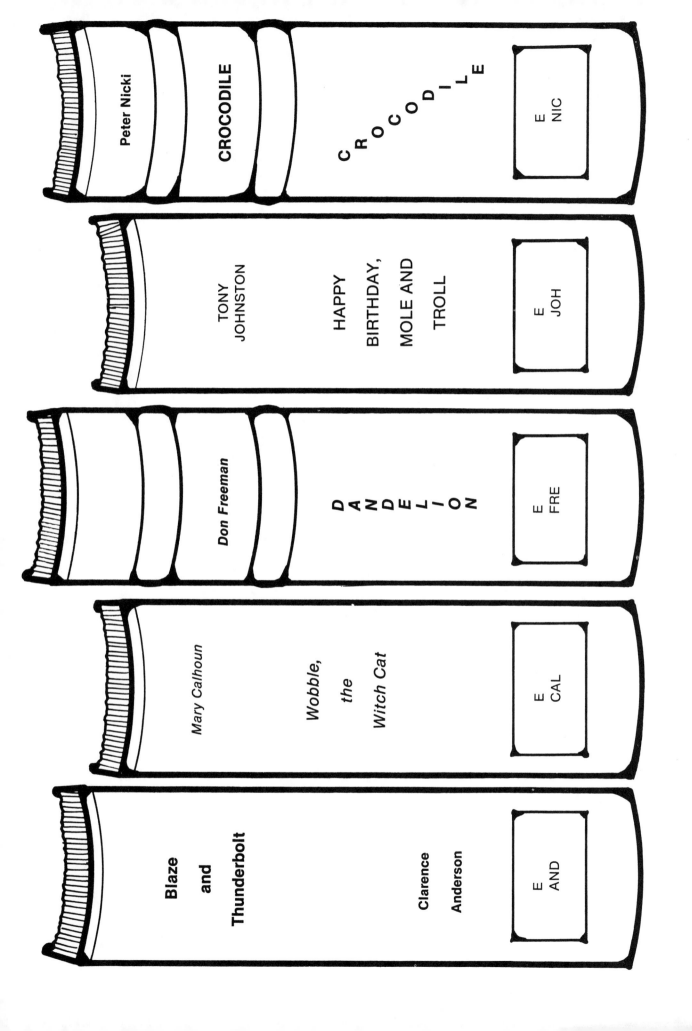

Answer Key

Starting from left to right, the correct order of these books is:

    Anderson—1
    Calhoun—2
    Freeman—3
    Johnston—4
    Nicki—5

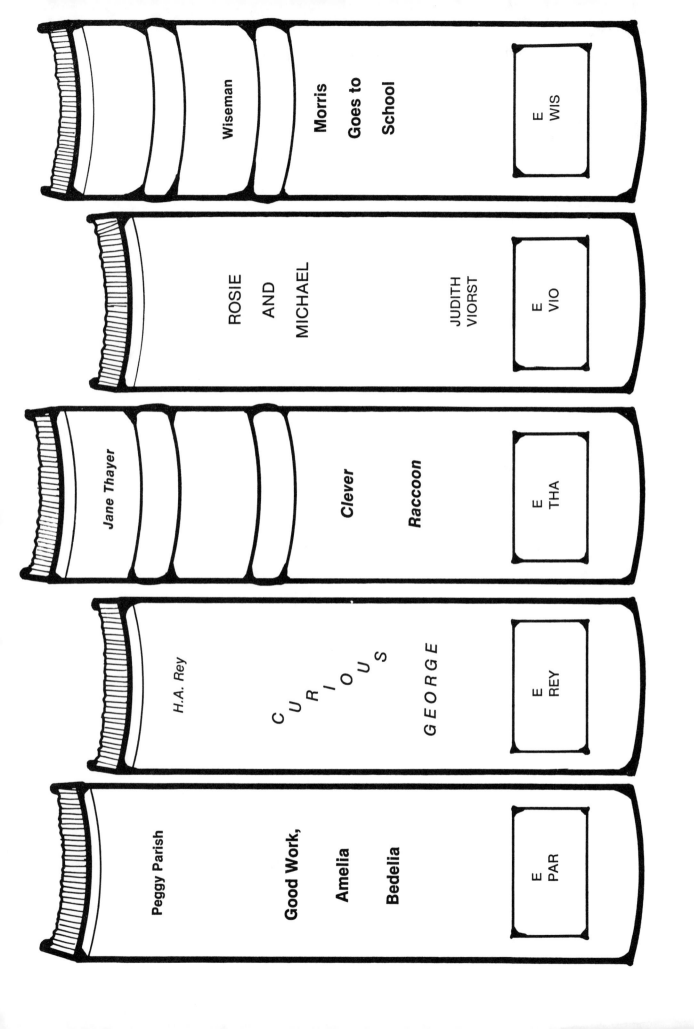

Peggy Parish

Good Work,
Amelia
Bedelia

E
PAR

H.A. Rey

CURIOUS GEORGE

E
REY

Jane Thayer

Clever

Raccoon

E
THA

ROSIE
AND
MICHAEL

JUDITH
VIORST

E
VIO

Wiseman

Morris
Goes to
School

E
WIS

Answer Key

Starting from left to right, the correct order of these books is:

    Parish—6
    Rey—7
    Thayer—8
    Viorst—9
    Wiseman—10

SET 3
ARRANGING FICTION BOOKS IN ORDER
BY AUTHOR'S LAST NAME, A–Z

Checklist of books used—15 titles in set

1.	F ADA	Adams, Richard G.	Watership Down
2.	F BAW	Bawden, Nina	Carrie's War
3.	F CLE	Cleary, Beverly	Henry Huggins
4.	F ECK	Eckert, Allan W.	Incident at Hawk's Hill
5.	F FLE	Fleischman, Albert S.	McBroom's Zoo
6.	F GEO	George, Jean Craighead	My Side of the Mountain
7.	F HEN	Henry, Marguerite	Little Fellow
8.	F KEY	Key, Alexander	Escape to Witch Mountain
9.	F LIT	Little, Jean	From Anna
10.	F MOW	Mowat, Farley	Owls in the Family
11.	F ODE	O'Dell, Scott	Sing Down the Moon
12.	F PAT	Paterson, Katherine	Bridge to Terabithia
13.	F SAC	Sachs, Marilyn	Veronica Ganz
14.	F VAN	Van Leeuwen, Jean	I Was a 98-Pound Duckling
15.	F WHI	White, Elwyn Broods	Trumpet of the Swan

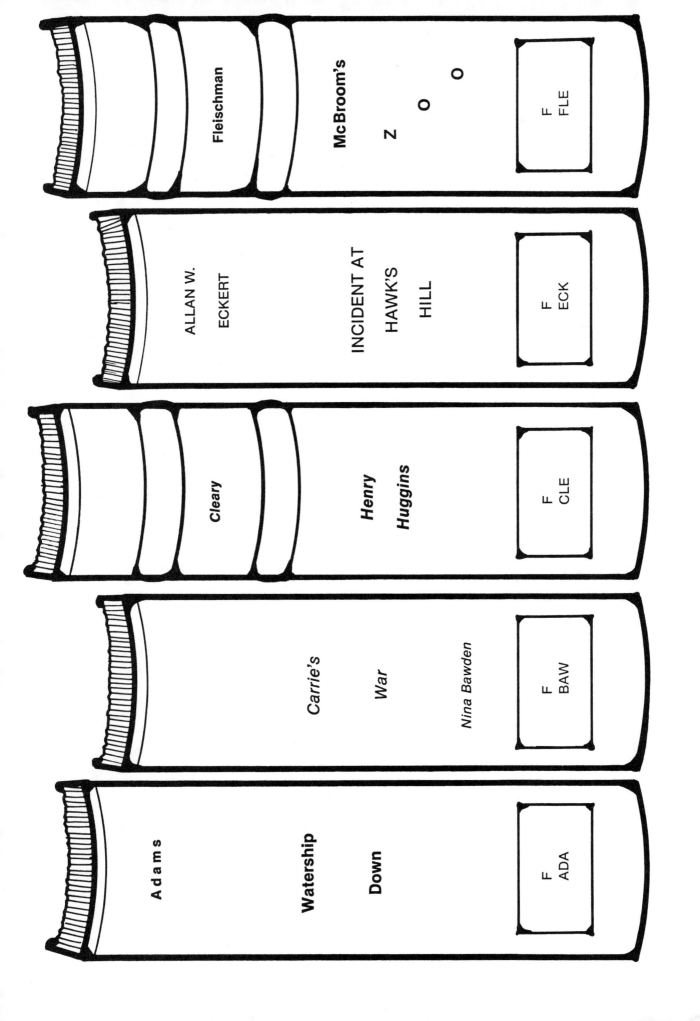

Answer Key

Starting from left to right, the correct order of these books is:

    Adams—1
    Bawden—2
    Cleary—3
    Eckert—4
    Fleischman—5

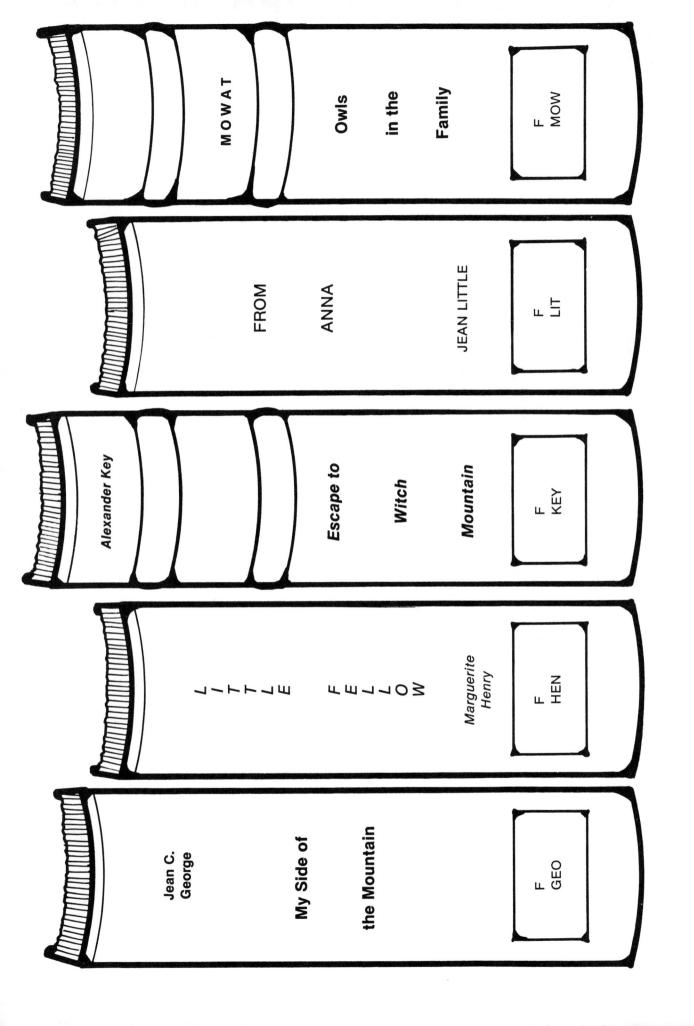

Answer Key

Starting from left to right, the correct order of these books is:

    George—6
    Henry—7
    Key—8
    Little—9
    Mowat—10

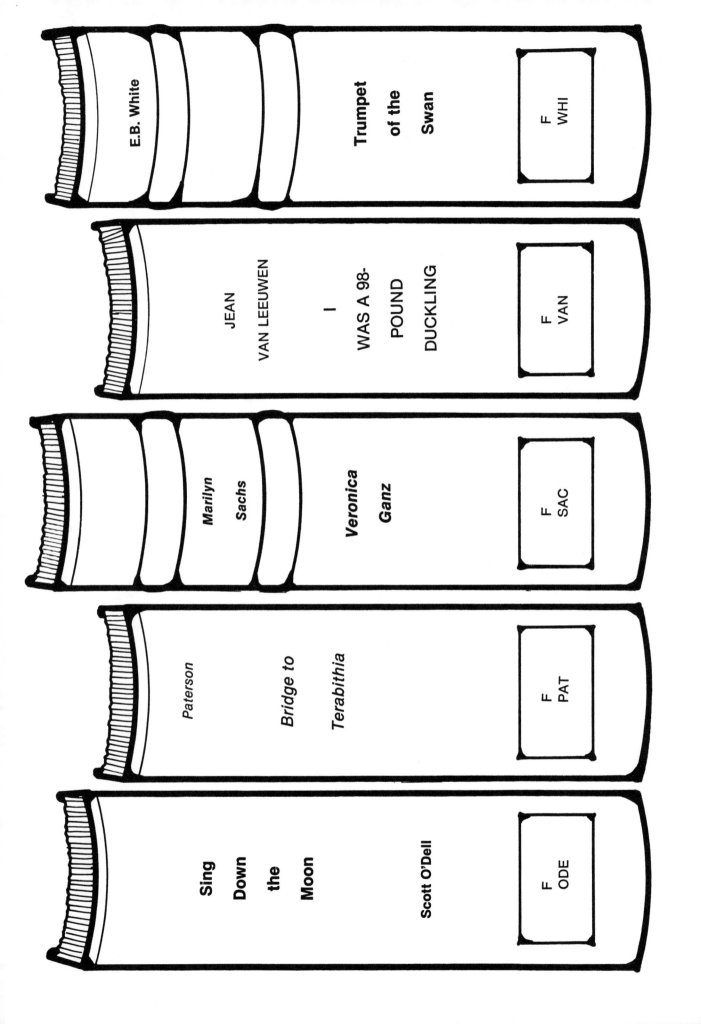

Answer Key

Starting from left to right, the correct order of these books is:

O'Dell—11
Paterson—12
Sachs—13
Van Leeuwen—14
White—15

SET 4
ARRANGING FICTION BOOKS IN ORDER
BY TITLE OF BOOK

Checklist of books used — 10 titles in set.

1.	F BLU	Are You There God? It's Me, Margaret.
2.	F BLU	Blubber
3.	F BLU	Deenie
4.	F BLU	Freckle Juice
5.	F BLU	Iggie's House
6.	F BLU	Otherwise Known As Sheila the Great
7.	F BLU	Superfudge
8.	F BLU	Tales of a Fourth Grade Nothing
9.	F BLU	Then Again, Maybe I Won't
10.	F BLU	Tiger Eyes

Author—Judy Blume
Must check the second letter of the first word in some titles.

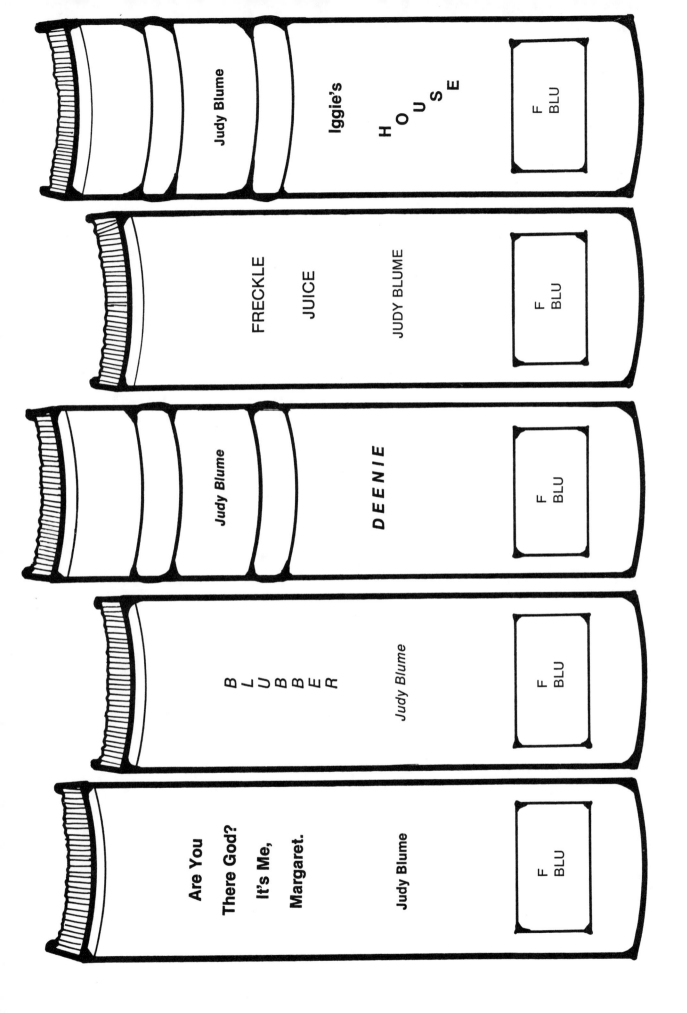

Answer Key

Starting from left to right, the correct order of these books is:

Are You There God? It's Me, Margaret—1
Blubber—2
Deenie—3
Freckle Juice—4
Iggie's House—5

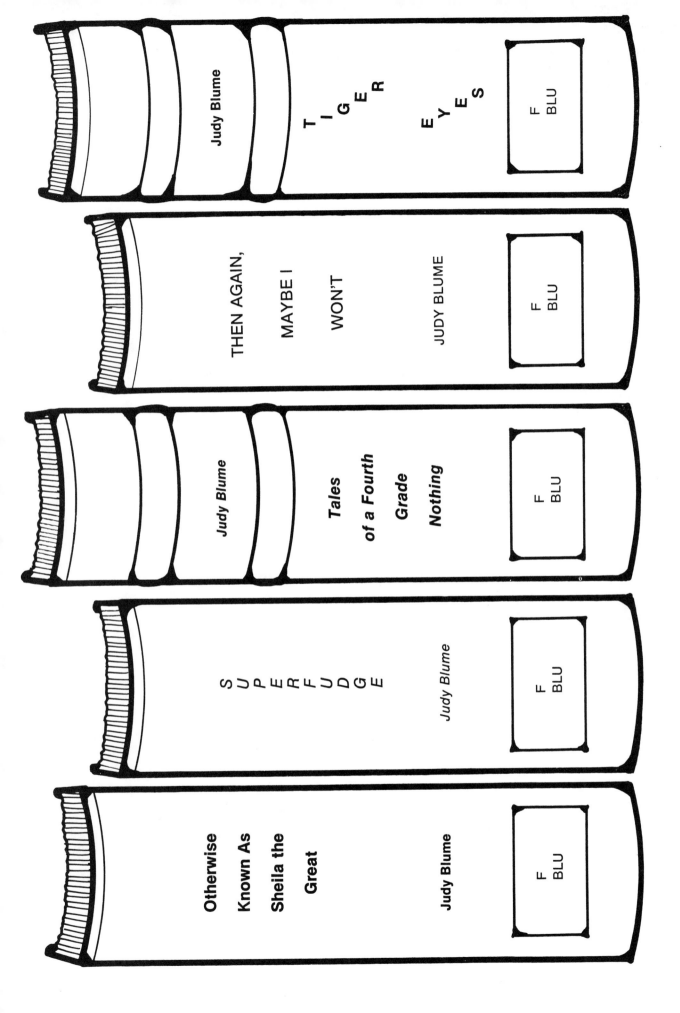

Otherwise
Known As
Sheila the
Great

Judy Blume

F
BLU

S
U
P
E
R
F
U
D
G
E

Judy Blume

F
BLU

Judy Blume

Tales
of a Fourth
Grade
Nothing

F
BLU

THEN AGAIN,

MAYBE I

WON'T

JUDY BLUME

F
BLU

Judy Blume

T
I
G
E
R

E
Y
E
S

F
BLU

Answer Key

Starting from left to right, the correct order of these books is:

    Otherwise Known As Sheila the Great—6
    Superfudge—7
    Tales of a Fourth Grade Nothing—8
    Then Again, Maybe I Won't—9
    Tiger Eyes—10

SET 5
ARRANGING FICTION BOOKS IN ORDER
BY TITLE OF BOOK

Checklist of books used — 10 titles in set.

	F BIA	
1.	BIA	Tizz
2.	BIA	Tizz and Company
3.	BIA	Tizz and the Fiesta
4.	BIA	Tizz at the Stampede
5.	BIA	Tizz in the Canadian Rockies
6.	BIA	Tizz on a Horse Farm
7.	BIA	Tizz on a Trail Ride
8.	BIA	Tizz Plays Santa Claus
9.	BIA	Tizz South of the Border
10.	BIA	Tizz Takes a Trip

Author—Elsa Bialk
Must check the second, third, or fourth word in the titles.

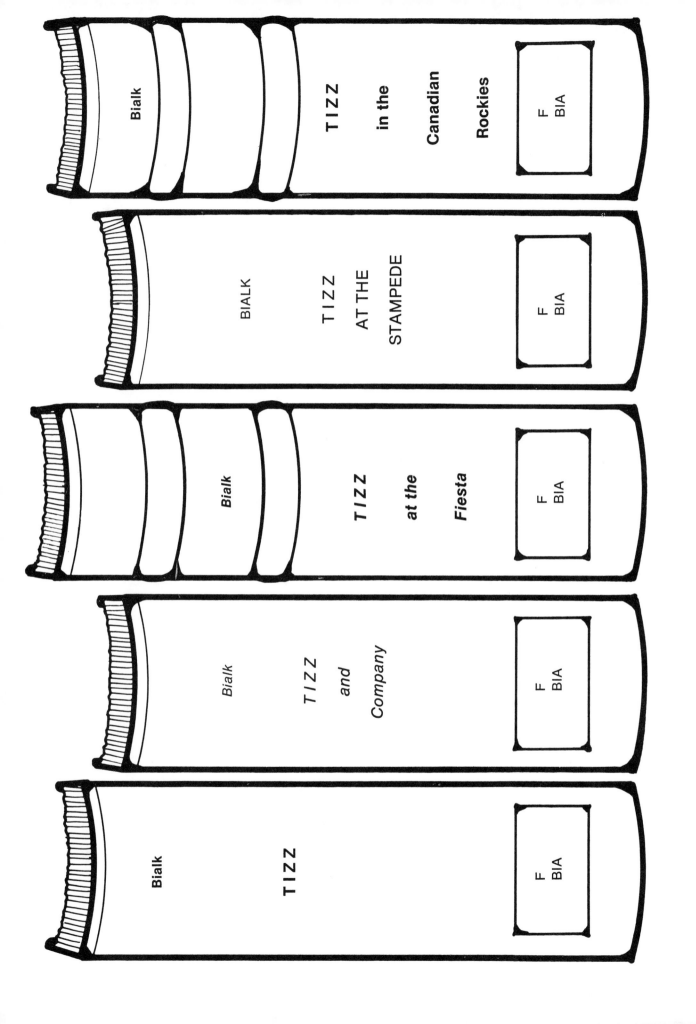

Answer Key

Starting from left to right, the correct order of these books is:
  Tizz—1
  Tizz and Company—2
  Tizz at the Fiesta—3
  Tizz at the Stampede—4
  Tizz in the Canadian Rockies—5

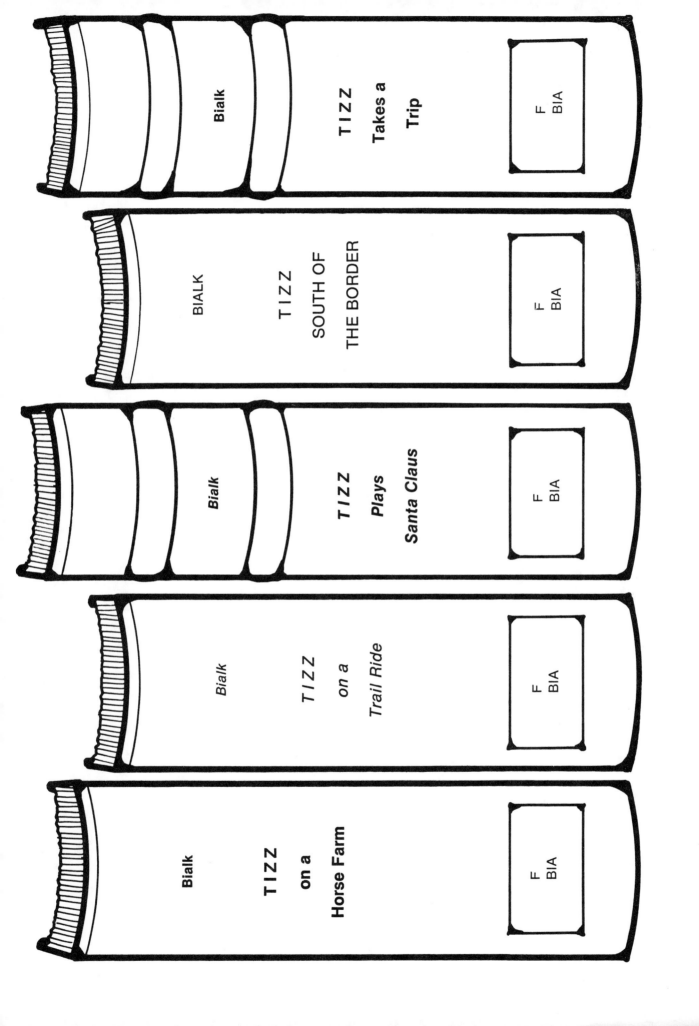

Answer Key

Starting from left to right, the correct order of these books is:

 Tizz on a Horse Farm—6
 Tizz on a Trail Ride—7
 Tizz Plays Santa Claus—8
 Tizz South of the Border—9
 Tizz Takes a Trip—10

SET 6

ARRANGING FICTION BOOKS IN ORDER
BY TITLE OF BOOK

Checklist of books used — 10 titles in set.

1.	F SOB	Encyclopedia Brown and the Case of the Midnight Visitor
2.	F SOB	Encyclopedia Brown and the Case of the Secret Pitch
3.	F SOB	Encyclopedia Brown, Boy Detective
4.	F SOB	Encyclopedia Brown Carries On
5.	F SOB	Encyclopedia Brown Finds the Clues
6.	F SOB	Encyclopedia Brown Keeps the Peace
7.	F SOB	Encyclopedia Brown Lends a Hand
8.	F SOB	Encyclopedia Brown Saves the Day
9.	F SOB	Encyclopedia Brown Solves Them All
10.	F SOB	Encyclopedia Brown Takes the Case

Author—Donald Sobol
Must check third, fourth, fifth, sixth, seventh, or eighth word in title.

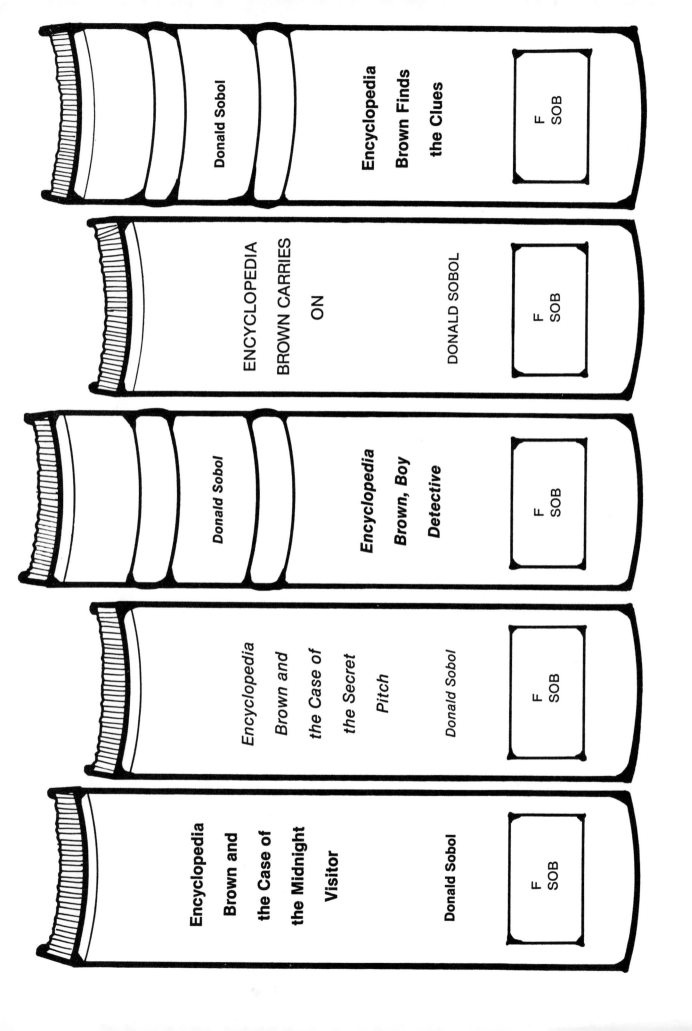

Answer Key

Starting from left to right, the correct order of these books is:

Encyclopedia Brown and the Case of the Midnight Visitor—1
Encyclopedia Brown and the Case of the Secret Pitch—2
Encyclopedia Brown, Boy Detective—3
Encyclopedia Brown Carries On—4
Encyclopedia Brown Finds the Clues—5

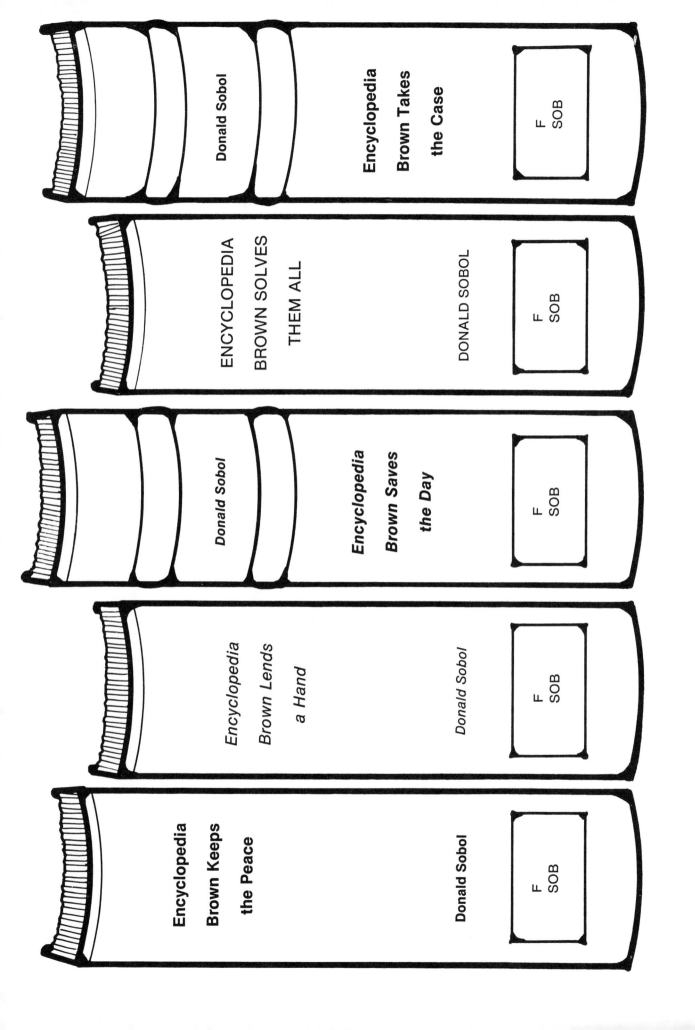

Answer Key

Starting from left to right, the correct order of these books is:

Encyclopedia Brown Keeps the Peace—6
Encyclopedia Brown Lends a Hand—7
Encyclopedia Brown Saves the Day—8
Encyclopedia Brown Solves Them All—9
Encyclopedia Brown Takes the Case—10

SET 7
ARRANGING FICTION BOOKS IN ORDER BY AUTHOR'S FIRST AND LAST NAME AND TITLE OF BOOK

Checklist of books used—15 titles in set.

1.	F SAC	Sachs, Marilyn	Bus Ride
2.	F SAC	Sachs, Marilyn	Secret Friend
3.	F SCH	Schwartz, Sheila	One Day You'll Go
4.	F SHA	Sharmat, Marjorie W.	Getting Something on Maggie Marmelstein
5.	F SMI	Smith, Dodie	The Hundred and One Dalmatians
6.	F SMI	Smith, Eunice	High-Heels for Jennifer
7.	F SOB	Sobol, Donald	Encyclopedia Brown
8.	F SPE	Speare, Elizabeth	Calico Capture
9.	F SPY	Spyri, Johanna	Heidi
10.	F STO	Stolz, Mary	A Dog on Barkham Street
11.	F STO	Stolz, Mary	Go and Catch a Flying Fish
12.	F STO	Stolz, Mary	Noonday Friends
13.	F STR	Stranger, Joyce	Circus Alone
14.	F SUT	Sutcliff, Rosemary	Road to Camlann
15.	F SWA	Swayze, Fred	Tonty of the Iron Hand

Must check the second or third letter in the author's last name.
Must check the first name of the author named Smith—Smith, Dodie; Smith, Eunice.
Must check the title of the book if there is more than one book by the same author.

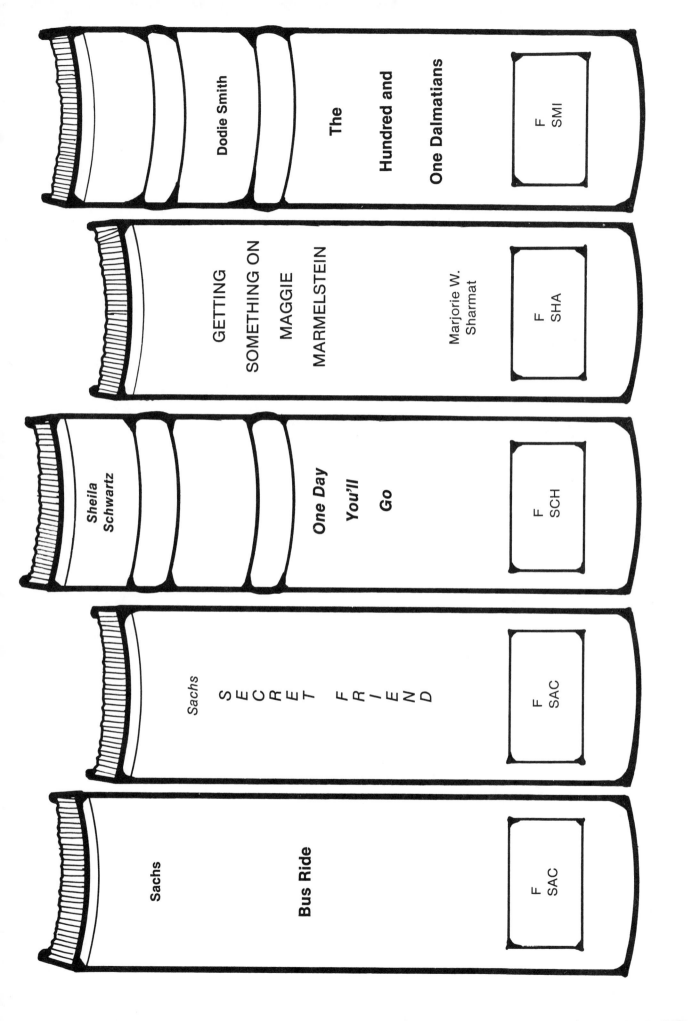

Dodie Smith

The

Hundred and

One Dalmatians

F
SMI

GETTING

SOMETHING ON

MAGGIE

MARMELSTEIN

Marjorie W.
Sharmat

F
SHA

Sheila
Schwartz

One Day

You'll

Go

F
SCH

Sachs

S
E
C
R
E
T

F
R
I
E
N
D

F
SAC

Sachs

Bus Ride

F
SAC

Answer Key

Starting from left to right, the correct order of these books is:

Bus Ride—1
Secret Friend—2
One Day You'll Go—3
Getting Something on Maggie Marmelstein—4
The Hundred and One Dalmatians—5

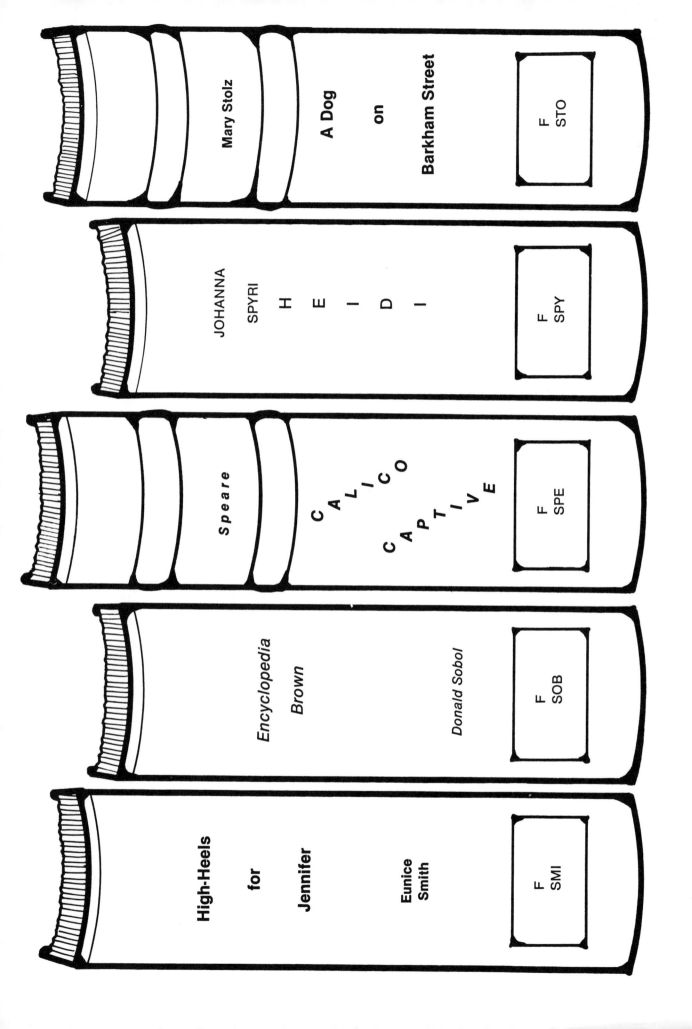

Answer Key

Starting from left to right, the correct order of these books is:

High-Heels for Jennifer—6
Encyclopedia Brown—7
Calico Capture—8
Heidi—9
A Dog on Barkham Street—10

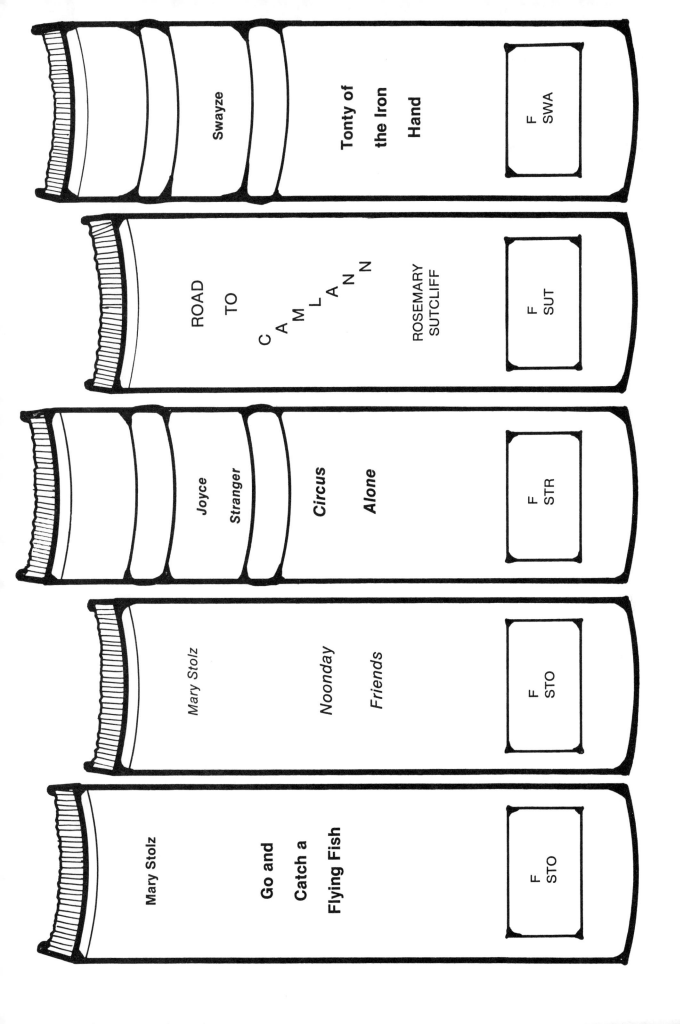

Answer Key

Starting from left to right, the correct order of these books is:

Go and Catch a Flying Fish—11
Noonday Friends—12
Circus Alone—13
Road to Camlann—14
Tonty of the Iron Hand—15

SET 8
ARRANGING EASY READING FICTION BOOKS IN ORDER BY TITLE OF BOOK

Checklist of books used — 15 titles in set.

1.	E SEU	Cat in the Hat
2.	E SEU	Dr. Seuss' Sleep Book
3.	E SEU	Foot Book
4.	E SEU	Fox in Socks
5.	E SEU	I Can Lick 30 Tigers Today
6.	E SEU	I Can Read With My Eyes Shut
7.	E SEU	Lorax
8.	E SEU	Oh the Thinks You Can Think
9.	E SEU	On Beyond Zebra
10.	E SEU	Scrambled Eggs Super
11.	E SEU	Shape of Me and Other Stuff
12.	E SEU	Sneetches and Other Stories
13.	E SEU	There's a Wocket in My Pocket
14.	E SEU	Thidwick, the Big-Hearted Moose
15.	E SEU	Yertle the Turtle

Author—Dr. Seuss
Must check the second or third word in some titles.
Must check the second or third letter of the first word in some titles.

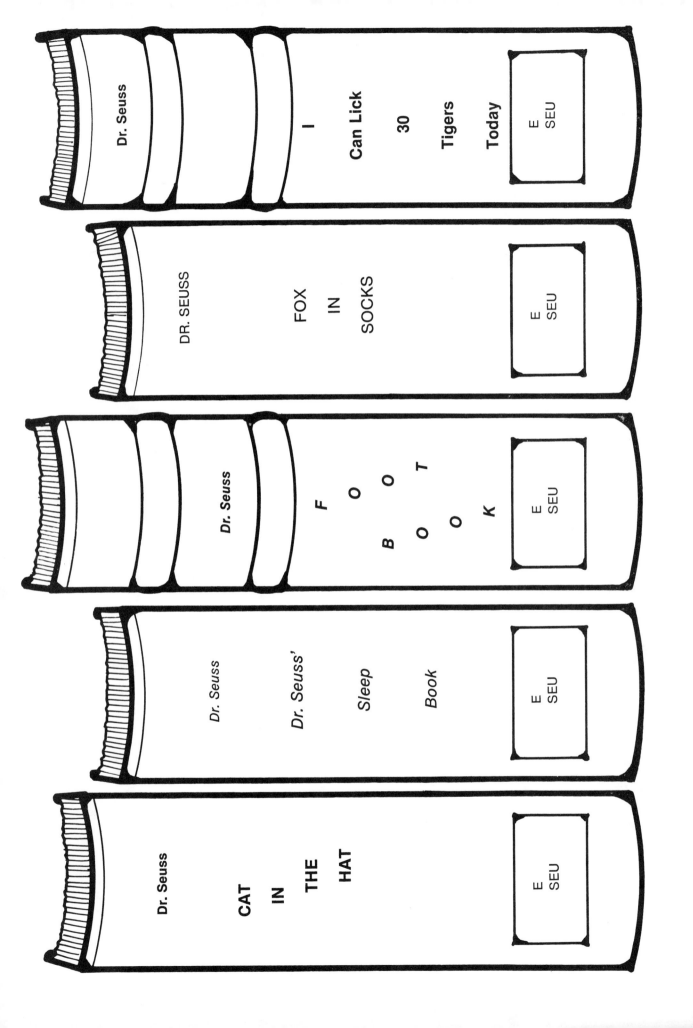

Answer Key

Starting from left to right, the correct order of these books is:

Cat in the Hat—1
Dr. Seuss's Sleep Book—2
Foot Book—3
Fox in Socks—4
I Can Lick 30 Tigers Today—5

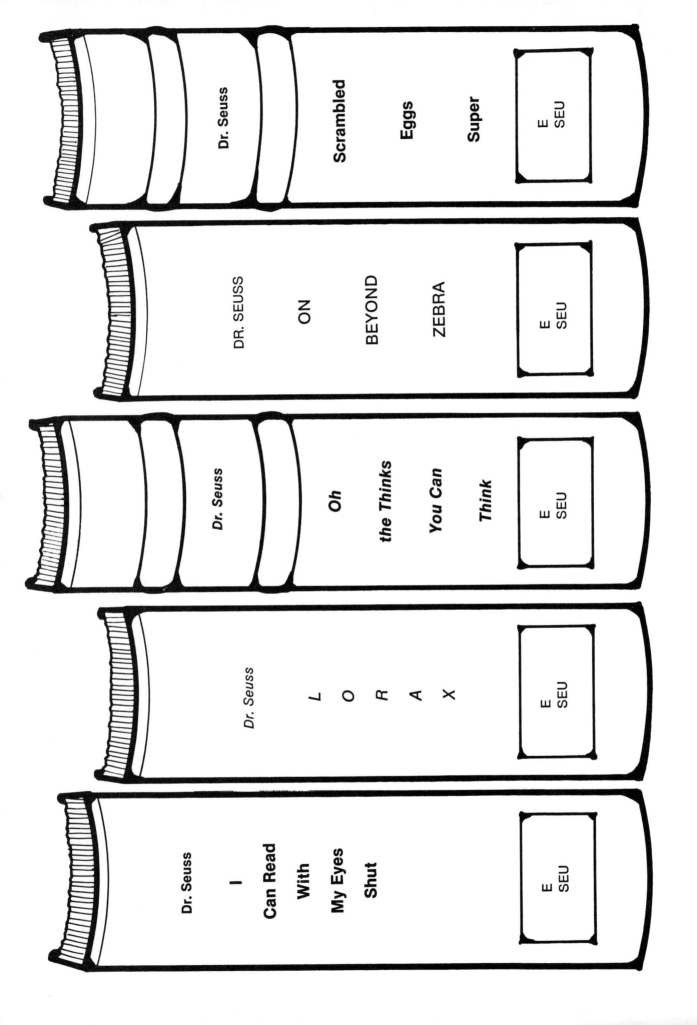

Answer Key

Starting from left to right, the correct order of these books is:
    I Can Read With My Eyes Shut—6
    Lorax—7
    Oh the Thinks You Can Think—8
    On Beyond Zebra—9
    Scrambled Eggs Super—10

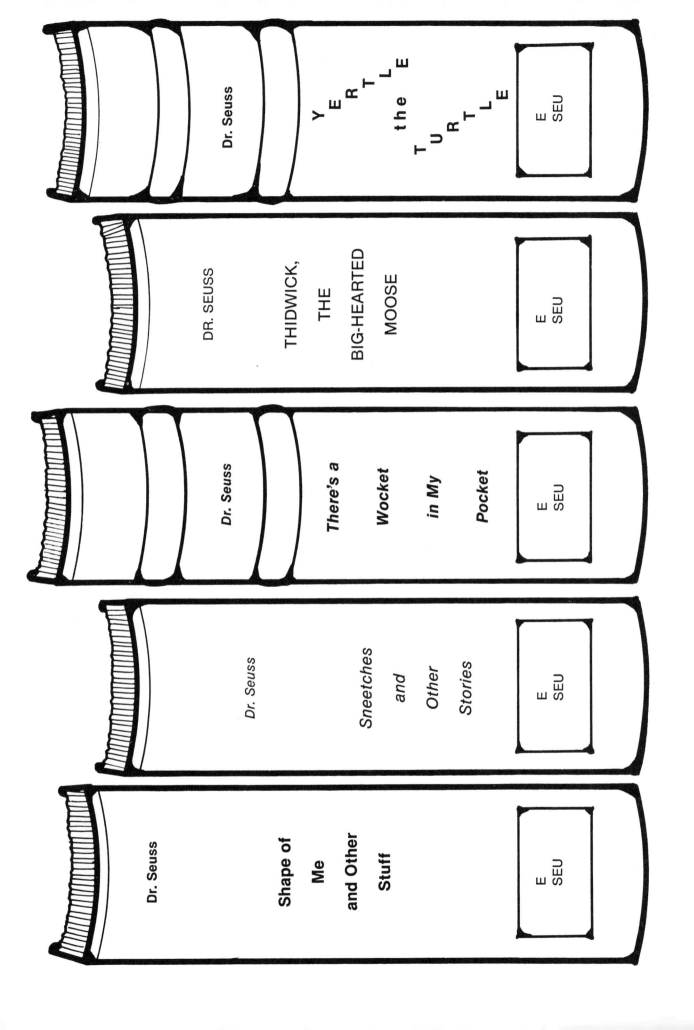

Dr. Seuss

YERTLE
the
TURTLE

E
SEU

DR. SEUSS

THIDWICK,
THE
BIG-HEARTED
MOOSE

E
SEU

Dr. Seuss

There's a
Wocket
in My
Pocket

E
SEU

Dr. Seuss

Sneetches
and
Other
Stories

E
SEU

Dr. Seuss

Shape of
Me
and Other
Stuff

E
SEU

Answer Key

Starting from left to right, the correct order of these books is:
    Shape of Me and Other Stuff—11
    Sneetches, and Other Stories—12
    There's a Wocket in My Pocket—13
    Thidwick, the Big-Hearted Moose—14
    Yertle the Turtle—15

SET 9

ARRANGING FICTION BOOKS IN ORDER BY AUTHOR'S FIRST AND LAST NAME AND TITLE OF BOOK

Checklist of books used — 15 titles in set.

1.	F HAA	Haas, Dorothy	Poppy and the Outdoors Cat
2.	F HAA	Haas, Jessie	Keeping Barney
3.	F HAH	Hahn, Mary	Time of the Witch
4.	F HAL	Hall, Donald	Man Who Lived Alone
5.	F HAL	Hall, Lynn	Danza!
6.	F HAL	Hall, Pam	On the Edge of the Eastern Ocean
7.	F HAN	Hanson, June	Winter of the Owl
8.	F HAR	Hardcastle, Michael	Fast From the Gate
9.	F HAR	Hardcastle, Michael	Team That Wouldn't Give In
10.	F HAR	Harris, Christie	Mystery at the Edge of Two Worlds
11.	F HAR	Harris, Dorothy J.	School Mouse
12.	F HAR	Harris, Dorothy	School Mouse and the Hamster
13.	F HAR	Harris, Geraldine	Seventh Gate
14.	F HAU	Haugaard, Erik C.	Boy's Will
15.	F HAY	Hayes, Sheila	No Autographs, Please

Must check the third letter in the author's last name.
Must check the first name of the authors named Haas, Hall, and Harris:

Haas, Dorothy; Haas, Jessie

Hall, Donald; Hall, Lyn; Hall, Pam

Harris, Christie; Harris, Dorothy; Harris, Geraldine.

Must check the title of the book if there is more than one book by the same author.

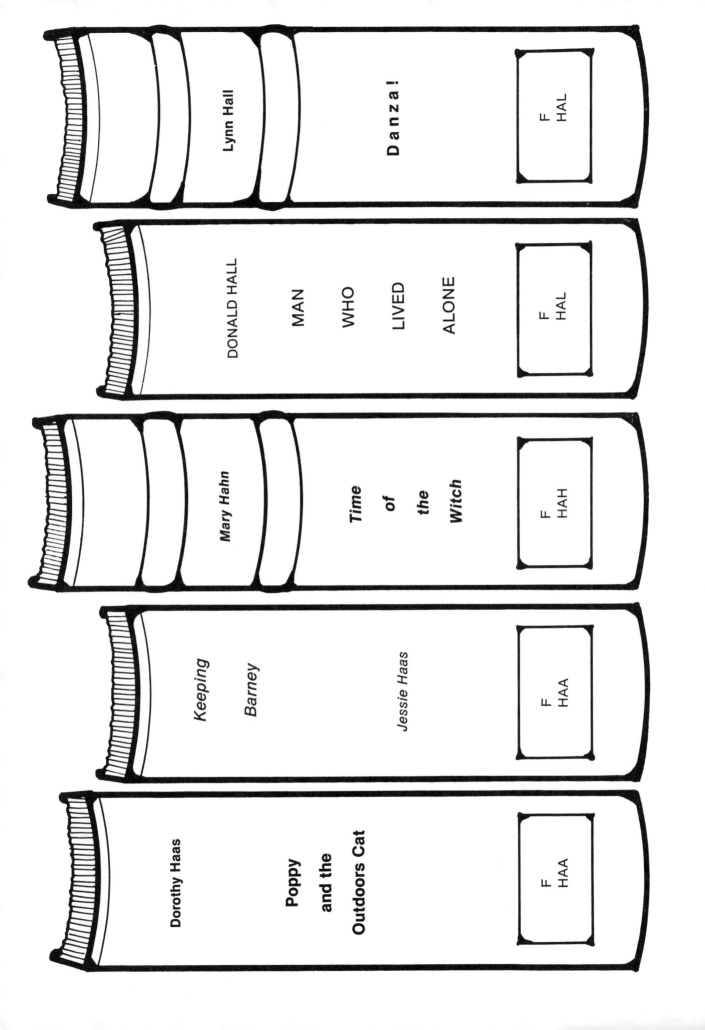

Answer Key

Starting from left to right, the correct order of these books is:

Poppy and the Outdoors Cat—1
Keeping Barney—2
Time of the Witch—3
Man Who Lived Alone—4
Danza!—5

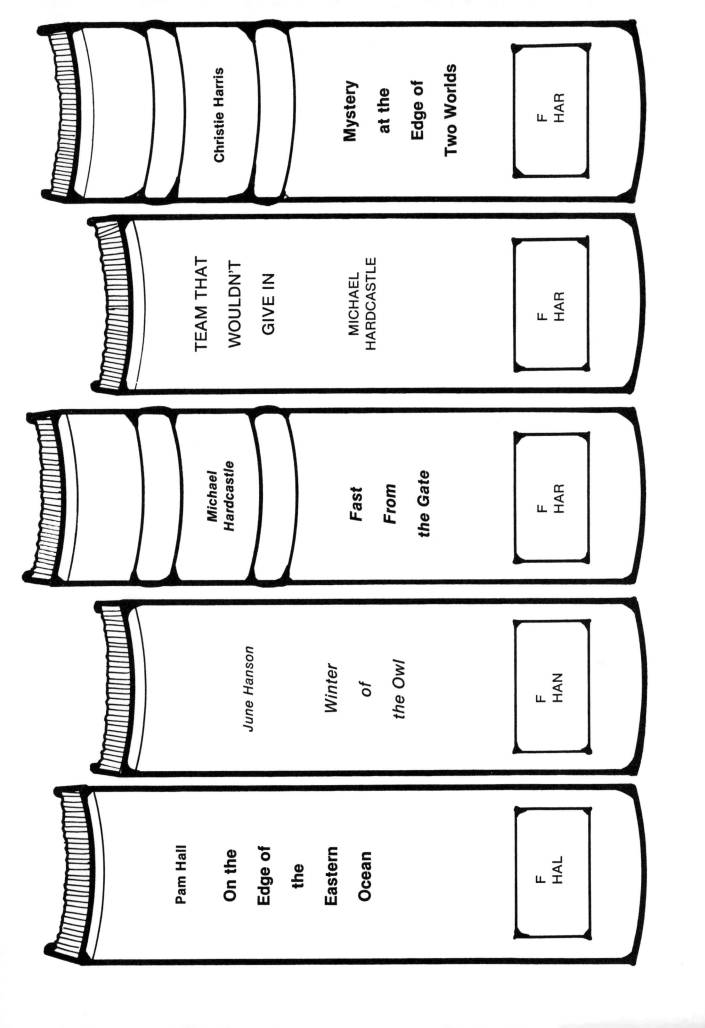

Answer Key

Starting from left to right, the correct order of these books is:

On the Edge of the Eastern Ocean—6
Winter of the Owl—7
Fast From the Gate—8
Team That Wouldn't Give In—9
Mystery at the Edge of Two Worlds—10

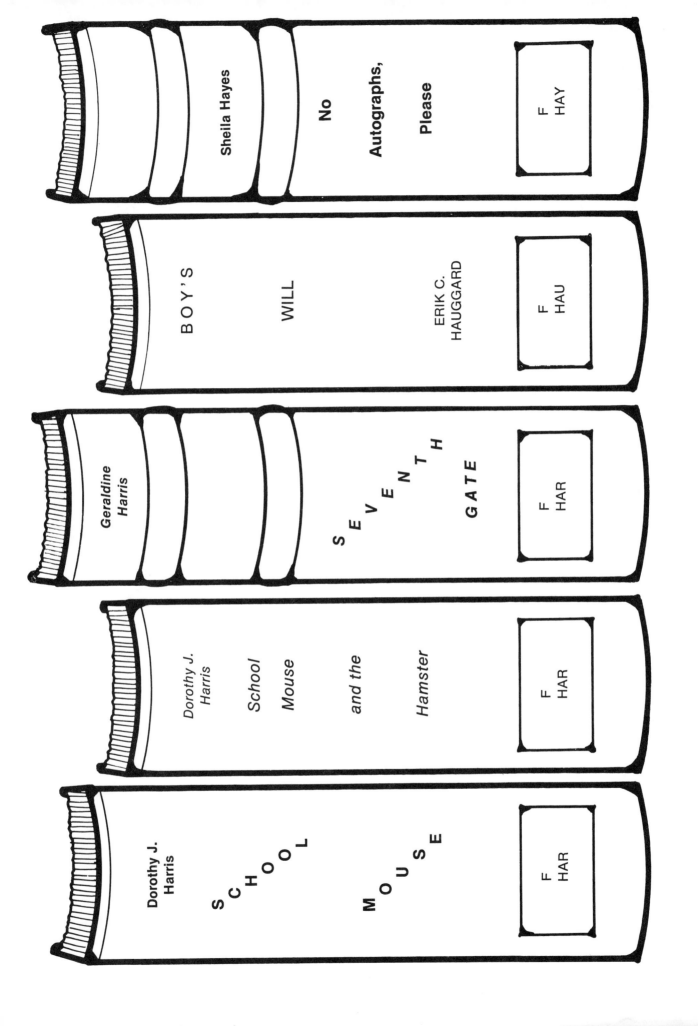

Answer Key

Starting from left to right, the correct order of these books is:
School Mouse—11
School Mouse and the Hamster—12
Seventh Gate—13
Boy's Will—14
No Autographs, Please—15

SET 10
ARRANGING FICTION BOOKS IN ORDER BY TITLE OF BOOK

Checklist of books used—15 titles in set.

1.	F CLE	Beezus and Ramona
2.	F CLE	Henry and Beezus
3.	F CLE	Henry and Ribsy
4.	F CLE	The Luckiest Girl
5.	F CLE	The Mouse and the Motorcycle
6.	F CLE	Otis Spofford
7.	F CLE	Ralph S. Mouse
8.	F CLE	Ramona and Her Father
9.	F CLE	Ramona and Her Mother
10.	F CLE	Ramona Forever
11.	F CLE	Ramona the Brave
12.	F CLE	Ramona the Pest
13.	F CLE	Ribsy
14.	F CLE	Sister of the Bride
15.	F CLE	Socks

Author—Beverly Cleary
Must check the first, second, third, or fourth word of the title.
Must check the second letter in the first word of some titles.

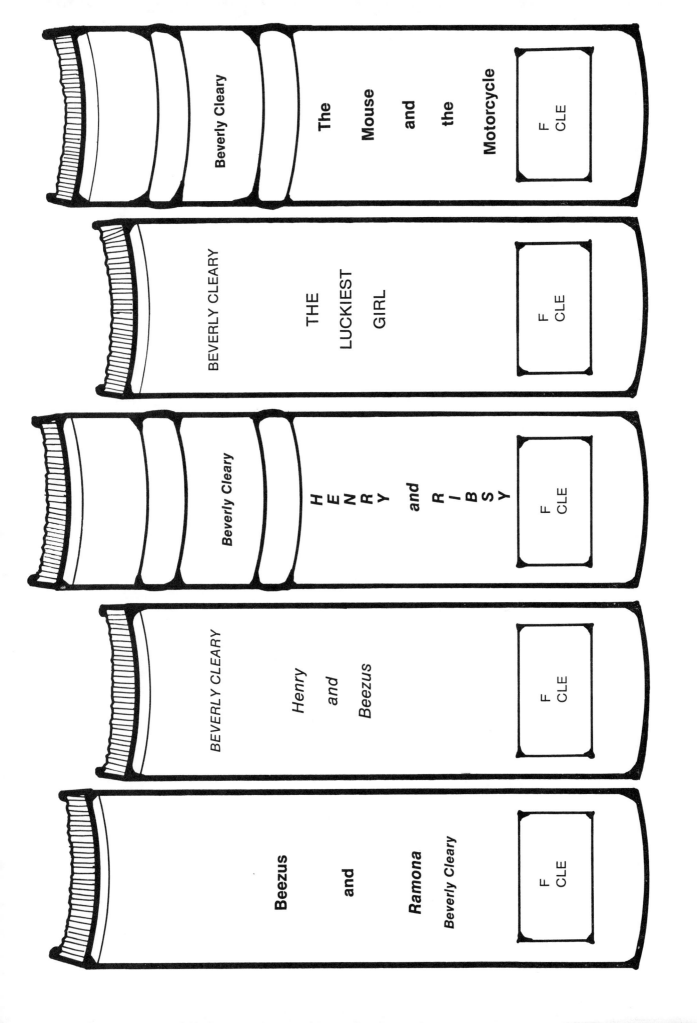

Answer Key

Starting from left to right, the correct order of these books is:
Beezus and Ramona—1
Henry and Beezus—2
Henry and Ribsy—3
The Luckiest Girl—4
The Mouse and the Motorcycle—5

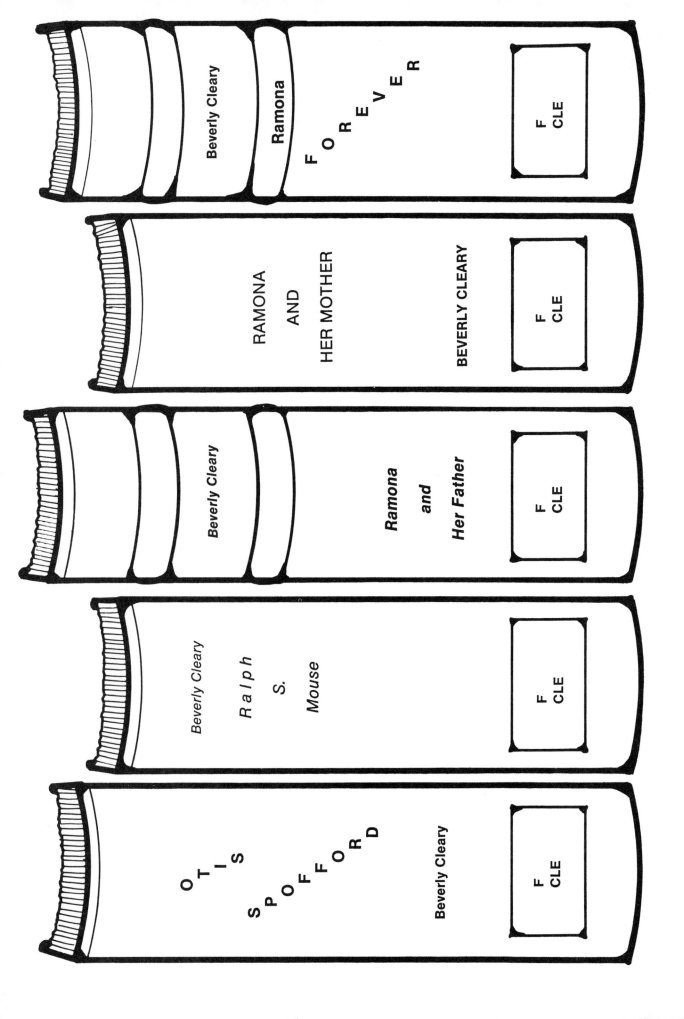

Answer Key

Starting from left to right, the correct order of these books is:

Otis Spofford—6
Ralph S. Mouse—7
Ramona and Her Father—8
Ramona and Her Mother—9
Ramona Forever—10

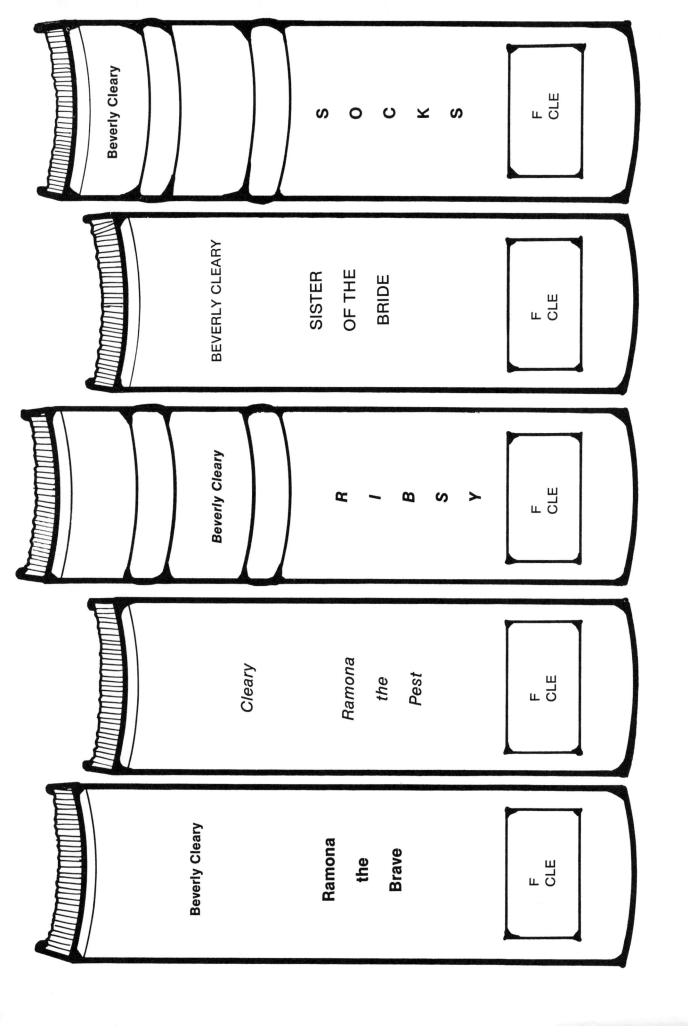

Answer Key

Starting from left to right, the correct order of these books is:

Ramona the Brave—11
Ramona the Pest—12
Ribsy—13
Sister of the Bride—14
Socks—15

Bookends

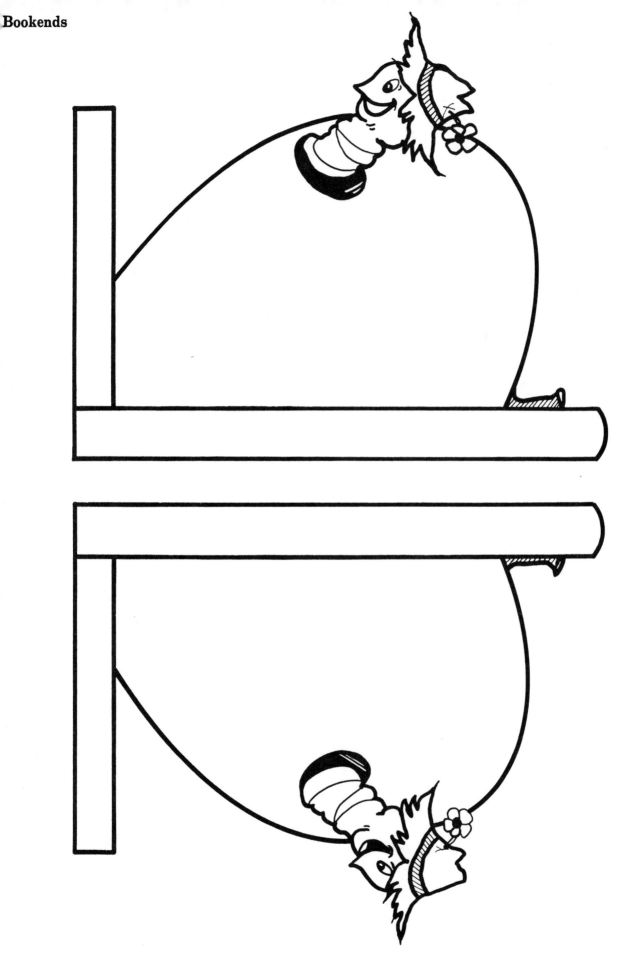

Color, mount on backing, and cut out to use with your sets of book spines.

ALPHA DOOBY NONFICTION ACTIVITIES

Practice in Arranging Nonfiction Books in Order

ALPHA DOOBY NONFICTION ACTIVITIES

Game Objectives:

1. To familiarize students with the arrangement of nonfiction books on library shelves.
2. To reinforce the ideas that:
   a. Nonfiction books are arranged on the shelves in order of call number and then alphabetically by the author's last name.
   b. If more than one book is written by the same author on the same subject, the books are arranged alphabetically by title.
   c. Sometimes books must be arranged by decimal point if the first part of the call number is similar. For instance, 796.4 would come before 796.8.
   d. Books on famous people with the call number 921 are arranged by call number and then alphabetically by the last name of the person the book is about. A book about Alexander Graham *Bell*, for example, is shelved before a book about Abraham *Lincoln.*
3. To make working with and learning about arranging nonfiction books in alphabetical order by authors' names, the person the book is about, call numbers, and titles of books an interesting, stimulating, and enjoyable activity.

Uses:

- These Alpha Dooby nonfiction activities can be used as a class activity, with each student working on his or her own set. The activities can also be used with small groups of students working together.
- Alpha Dooby Nonfiction Activities can be used to train library club members in all the aspects of shelving nonfiction books in correct alphabetical order.
- The activities can be used to introduce, reinforce, or culminate lessons taught on any aspect of alphabetical arrangement in library-related activities.
- The activities can be used in a library, a classroom, or any activity center.

Materials Needed:

- Scissors
- Copier machine
- 10 book card pockets, 10 folders, or 10 envelopes
- Marking pens
- *optional:* Clear self-stick vinyl
- *optional:* Tagboard
- *optional:* Glue

Construction Directions:

1. Make the number of copies of each set you need for the students and write the numbers 1 through 10 or 1 through 15 on the backs of the book spines.

2. Cut out each book spine and let the students color and decorate them if desired. (*Note:* For more durability, mount the spines onto tagboard and then cover with clear self-stick vinyl. Remember to print the numbers on the spines before covering them with the vinyl and cutting out.)

3. Explain to the students the instructions for using each set of book spines. Write these instructions on the card pocket (or folder or envelope) for each set (see the sample in the illustration):

   Set 1—Same call numbers—398.2

    Arrange nonfiction books in alphabetical order by author's last name, A–Z (10 titles).

   Set 2—Same call numbers—821

    Arrange nonfiction books in alphabetical order by author's last name, A–S. If some books are by same author, arrange them by the title of book (15 titles).

   Set 3—Same call numbers—371.42

    Arrange nonfiction books in alphabetical order by author's last name, A–Z. If some books are by same author, arrange them by the title of book—5th word (15 titles).

   Set 4—Different call numbers—500s

    Arrange in numerical order by call numbers, 500–568 (10 titles).

   Set 5—Different call numbers—973s

    Arrange in numerical order by decimal point (10 titles).

   Set 6—Different call numbers—300s

    Arrange in numerical order by call numbers, 301 through 395 (15 titles).

   Set 7—Different call numbers—636s

    Arrange in numerical order by decimal point. If they have same call number, arrange the books by the author's last name (15 titles).

   Set 8—Same call numbers—921

    Arrange by the last name of the *person* the book is about (10 titles).

   Set 9—Same call numbers—921

    Arrange by the last name of the *person* book is about. Arrange them by author's last name if more than one book about the same person (15 titles).

   Set 10—Different call numbers—790s

    Arrange the books in numerical order by call number and decimal point (15 titles).

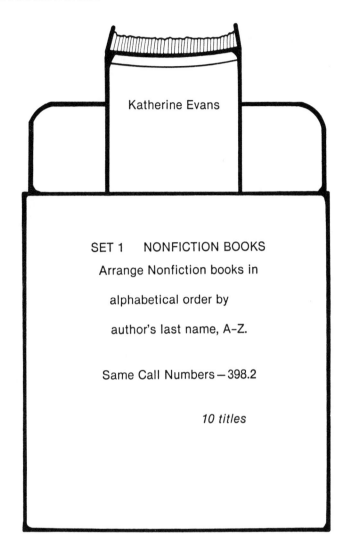

Katherine Evans

SET 1   NONFICTION BOOKS

Arrange Nonfiction books in

alphabetical order by

author's last name, A–Z.

Same Call Numbers – 398.2

10 titles

4. Make enough copies of the bookends so that students can color, laminate, and cut them out when using a set of book spines. The bookends can then be placed in the card pocket along with the spines.

Playing Suggestions:

1. Shuffle the book spines in each set so that they are not in the correct order.
2. Have the students arrange the spines in the order they feel is correct. Then ask them to turn each book spine over to check the answers. If the spines have been arranged correctly, the numbers 1 through 10 or 1 through 15 will be in order. If not, let the students try to determine what is incorrect. Then shuffle the book spines and try again.

3. When the students are finished working with a set, make sure all book spines are returned to the proper folder, envelope, or card pocket.

4. Have students work with as many different sets as possible so that skills in all aspects of alphabetical arrangement of NONFICTION books will be learned or reinforced.

Setting Up Activity Centers:

1. Place at least *one* copy of each set in a small box for use in the center, and have each set in a card pocket, envelope, or folder. (You might want to have FICTION and NONFICTION sets in different boxes.)

2. Type or write the instructions on the front of each box, as shown in the sample illustration:

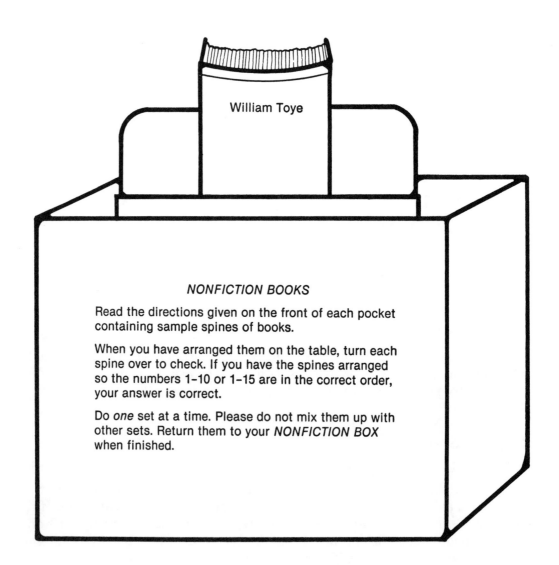

William Toye

NONFICTION BOOKS

Read the directions given on the front of each pocket containing sample spines of books.

When you have arranged them on the table, turn each spine over to check. If you have the spines arranged so the numbers 1–10 or 1–15 are in the correct order, your answer is correct.

Do *one* set at a time. Please do not mix them up with other sets. Return them to your *NONFICTION BOX* when finished.

General Rules for Arranging Nonfiction Books in Order:

1. All nonfiction or factual books receive a Dewey Decimal classification number called a *call number*. The call number for the subject "fairy tales," for example, is 398.2; therefore, any book on that subject would use the same call number.

2. Nonfiction books are arranged on the shelf first by their call number. Thus, all books numbered 398.2 come before books numbered 398.8.

3. All nonfiction books with the same call number will then be arranged on the shelves in alphabetical order according to the author's last name. Here is an example:

Andersen	Grimm	Southgate
398.2	398.2	398.2
AND	GRI	SOU

4. When arranging nonfiction books that have the same number and are written by the same author, you arrange the books in alphabetical order by title. Remember that "A," "An," and "The" at the beginning of a title do not count. Thus, *Thumbelina* by Hans Christian Andersen would come before *The Wild Swans*.

5. Biography books in the nonfiction section get special treatment. A biography is the story of a person's life, so the Dewey number includes the first three letters of the last name of the person the book is about. For example, the biography *Abe Lincoln Grows Up* by Carl Sandburg may have this call number:

921
LIN
San

Other variations used by some libraries may be:

921	921	921
LIN	B	LIN
		SAN

ALPHA DOOBY
NONFICTION
ACTIVITIES

Book Spine Sets

SET 1
ARRANGING NONFICTION BOOKS IN ORDER

Checklist of books used—10 titles in set.

1.	398.2 AND	Andersen, Hans C.	The Ugly Duckling
2.	398.2 CLE	Cleaver, Nancy	How the Chipmunk Got Its Stripes
3.	398.2 EVA	Evans, Katherine	Boy Who Cried Wolf
4.	398.2 GRI	Grimm, Brothers	The Shoemaker and the Elves
5.	398.2 KEN	Kent, Jack	Fables of Aesop
6.	398.2 MOS	Mosel, Arlene	Tikki Tikki Tembo
7.	398.2 POT	Potter, Grace E.	Giants and Fairies
8.	398.2 TOY	Toye, William	The Fire Stealer
9.	398.2 UCH	Uchida, Yoshiko	The Dancing Kettle
10.	398.2 ZEM	Zemach, Harve	Salt

Same Call Numbers—398.2
Arrange the authors' last names in order, A to Z.

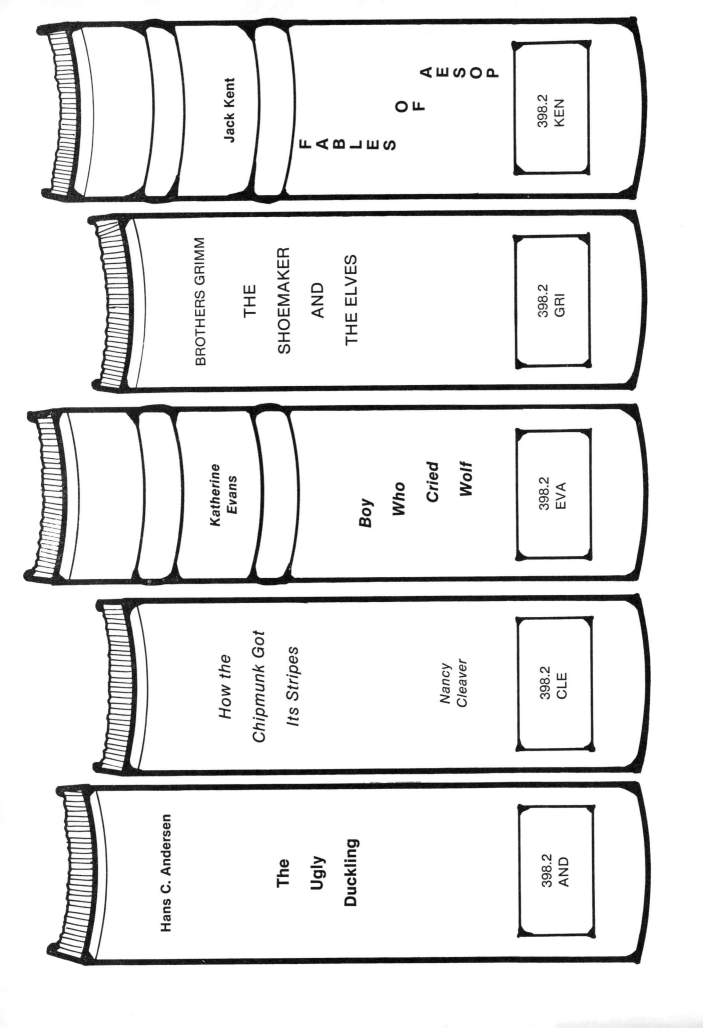

Answer Key

Starting from left to right, the correct order of these books is:

      Anderson—1

      Cleaver—2

      Evans—3

      Grimm—4

      Kent—5

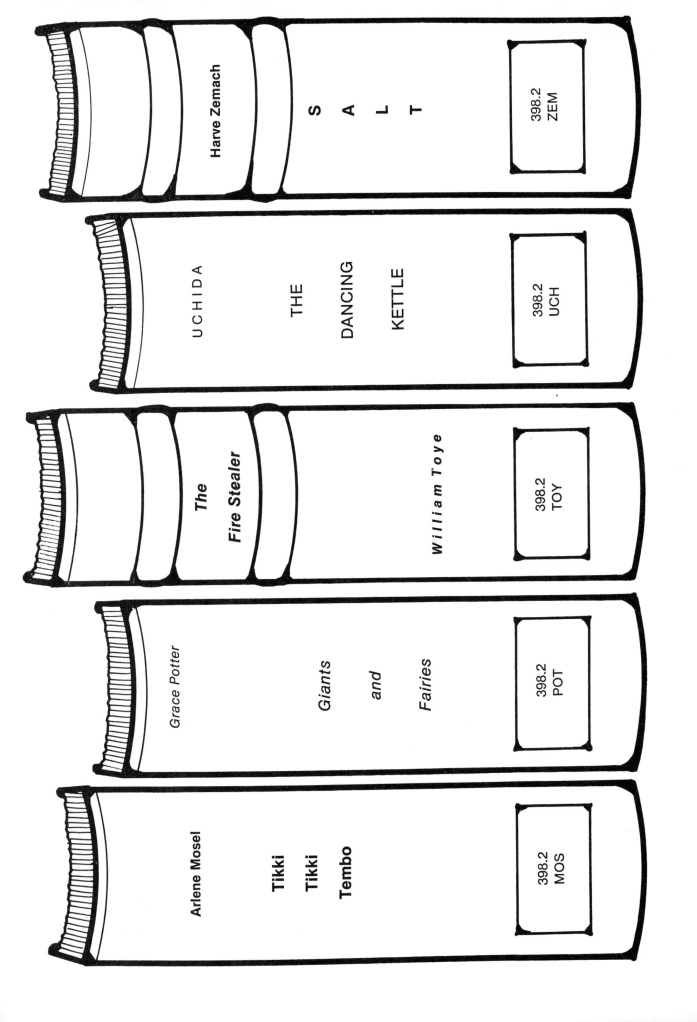

Answer Key

Starting from left to right, the correct order of these books is:

    Mosel—6
    Potter—7
    Toye—8
    Uchida—9
    Zemach—10

SET 2

ARRANGING NONFICTION BOOKS IN ORDER

Checklist of books used — 15 titles in set.

1.	821 ATW	Atwood, Ann	Haiku: The Mood of the Earth
2.	821 BAR	Barrows, Marjorie	Read Aloud Poems
3.	821 BRE	Brewster, Elizabeth	Sunrise North
4.	821 DOA	Doane, Pelagie	A Small Child's Book of Verse
5.	821 FIE	Field, Eugene	Poems of Childhood
6.	821 JOH	Johnson, E. Pauline	Flint and Feather
7.	821 LEE	Lee, Dennis	Alligator Pie
8.	821 NAS	Nash, Ogden	Moon Is Shining Bright As Day
9.	821 ONE	O'Neill, Mary	Hailstones and Halibut Bones
10.	821 PAR	Parker, E.W.	The Road Ahead
11.	821 SAN	Sandburg, Carl	Wind Song
12.	821 SER	Service, Robert	Songs of a Sourdough
13.	821 SIL	Silverstein, Shel	A Light in the Attic
14.	821 SIL	Silverstein, Shel	Where the Sidewalk Ends
15.	821 STE	Stevenson, Robert L.	A Child's Garden of Verses

Same Call Numbers—821
Arrange the authors' last names in order, A to S.
If the books are by the same author, arrange the titles in alphabetical order.

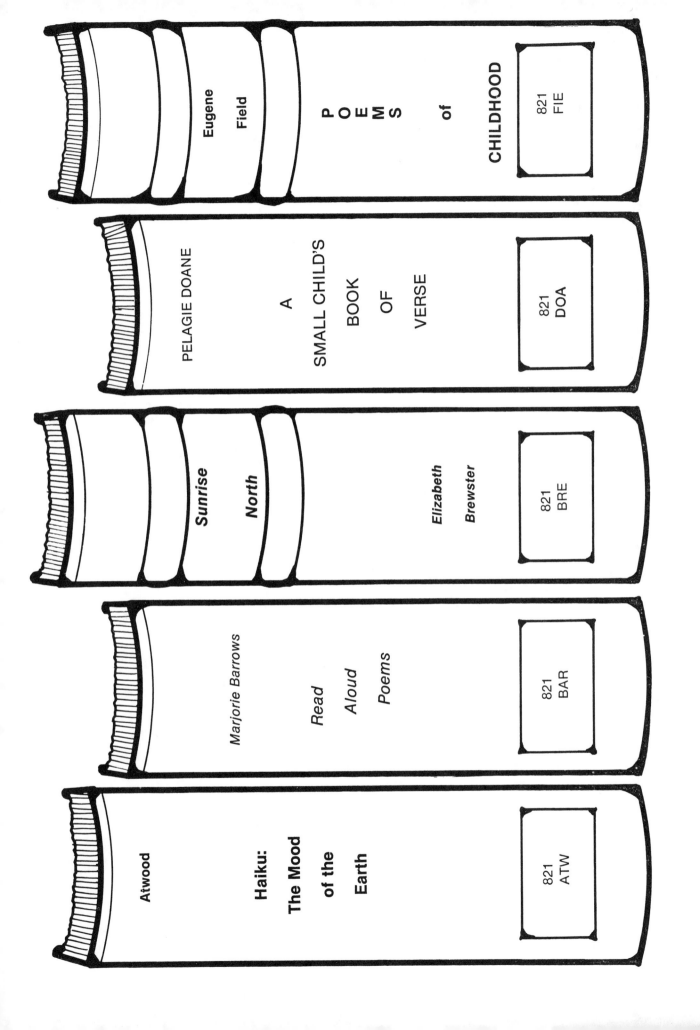

Eugene Field

P
O
E
M
S

of

CHILDHOOD

821
FIE

PELAGIE DOANE

A
SMALL CHILD'S

BOOK

OF

VERSE

821
DOA

Sunrise

North

Elizabeth

Brewster

821
BRE

Marjorie Barrows

Read

Aloud

Poems

821
BAR

Atwood

Haiku:
The Mood

of the

Earth

821
ATW

Answer Key

Starting from left to right, the correct order of these books is:
    Atwood—1
    Barrows—2
    Brewster—3
    Doane—4
    Field—5

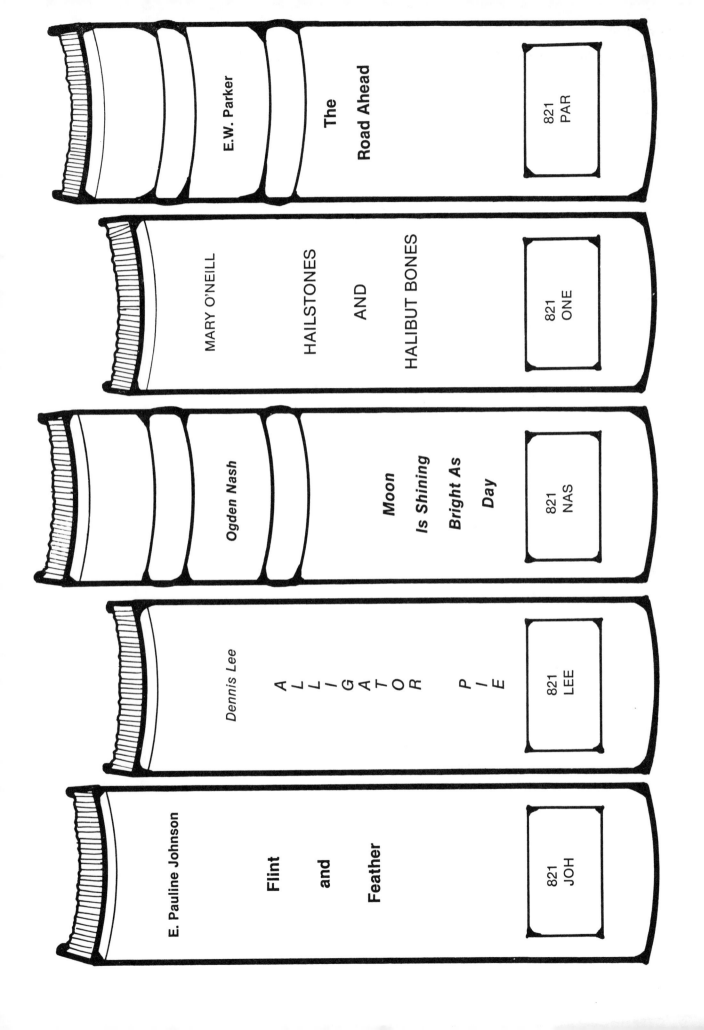

Answer Key

Starting from left to right, the correct order of these books is:

    Johnson—6
    Lee—7
    Nash—8
    O'Neill—9
    Parker—10

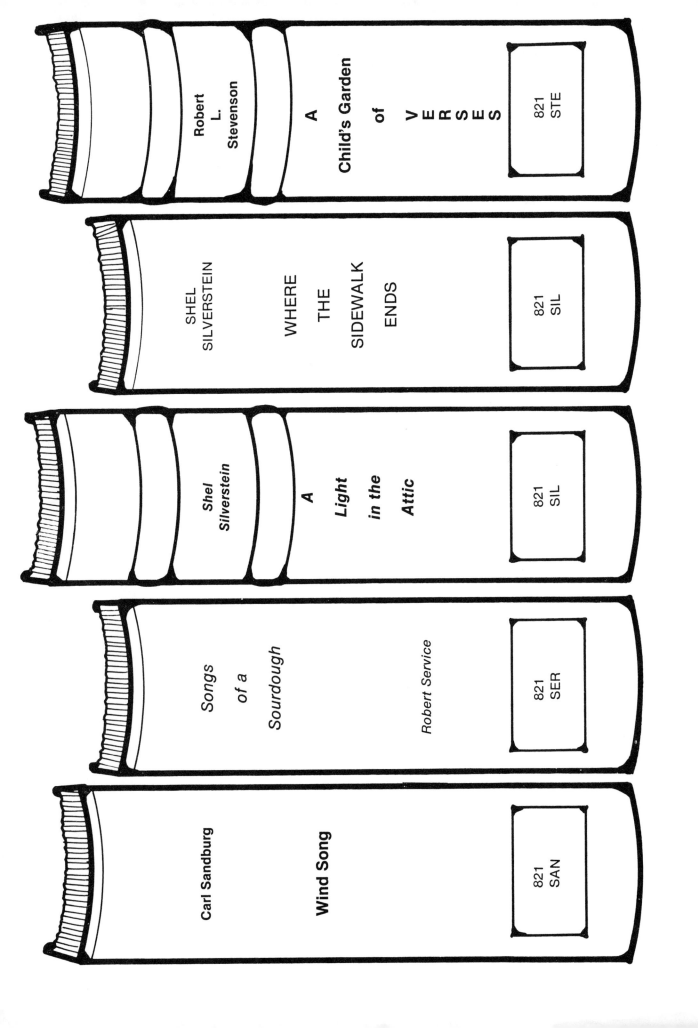

Answer Key

Starting from left to right, the correct order of these books is:
Sandburg—11
Service—12
Silverstein (*A Light in the Attic*)—13
Silverstein (*Where the Sidewalk Ends*)—14
Stevenson—15

SET 3
ARRANGING NONFICTION BOOKS IN ORDER

Checklist of books used — 15 titles in set.

1.	371.42 ALL	Allinson, Beverley	Myra Builds a House
2.	371.42 BAK	Baker, Eugene	I Want to Be a Bank Teller
3.	371.42 BAK	Baker, Eugene	I Want to Be a Football Player
4.	371.42 BAK	Baker, Eugene	I Want to Be a Lawyer
5.	371.42 BAK	Baker, Eugene	I Want to Be a Tennis Player
6.	371.42 GRE	Greene, Carla	I Want to Be a Dentist
7.	371.42 GRE	Greene, Carla	I Want to Be a Fireman
8.	371.42 GRE	Greene, Carla	I Want to Be a Musician
9.	371.42 GRE	Greene, Carla	I Want to Be a Nurse
10.	371.42 GRE	Greene, Carla	I Want to Be a Pilot
11.	371.42 GRE	Greene, Carla	I Want to Be a Ship Captain
12.	371.42 GRE	Greene, Carla	I Want to Be a Teacher
13.	371.42 LIE	Liebers, Arthur	You Can Be a Plumber
14.	371.42 SIL	Silvers, Brenda	Let's Pretend We Work in a Bank
15.	371.42 WIL	Wilkinson, Jean	Come to Work With Us in a TV Station

Same Call Numbers—371.42
Arrange the authors' last names in order.
If the books are by the same author, arrange the titles in order (6th word).

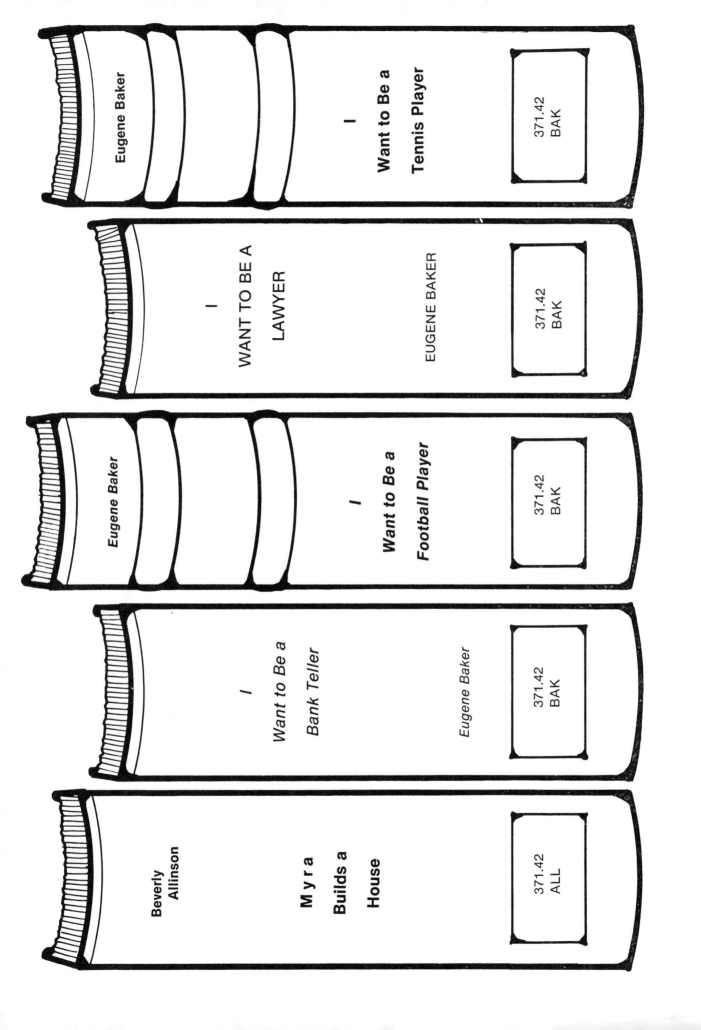

Answer Key

Starting from left to right, the correct order of these books is:

    Allinson—1

    Baker (*I Want to Be a Bank Teller*)—2

    Baker (*I Want to Be a Football Player*)—3

    Baker (*I Want to Be a Lawyer*)—4

    Baker (*I Want to Be a Tennis Player*)—5

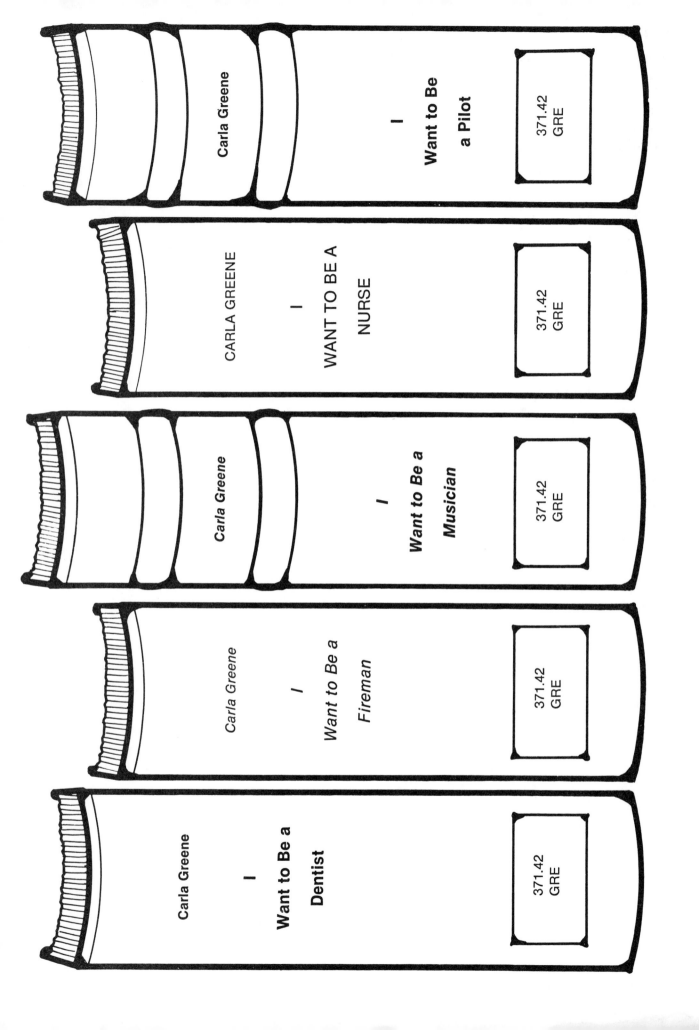

Answer Key

Starting from left to right, the correct order of these books is:

    Greene (*I Want to Be a Dentist*)—6
    Greene (*I Want to Be a Fireman*)—7
    Greene (*I Want to Be a Musician*)
    Greene (*I Want to Be a Nurse*)—9
    Greene (*I Want to Be a Pilot*)—10

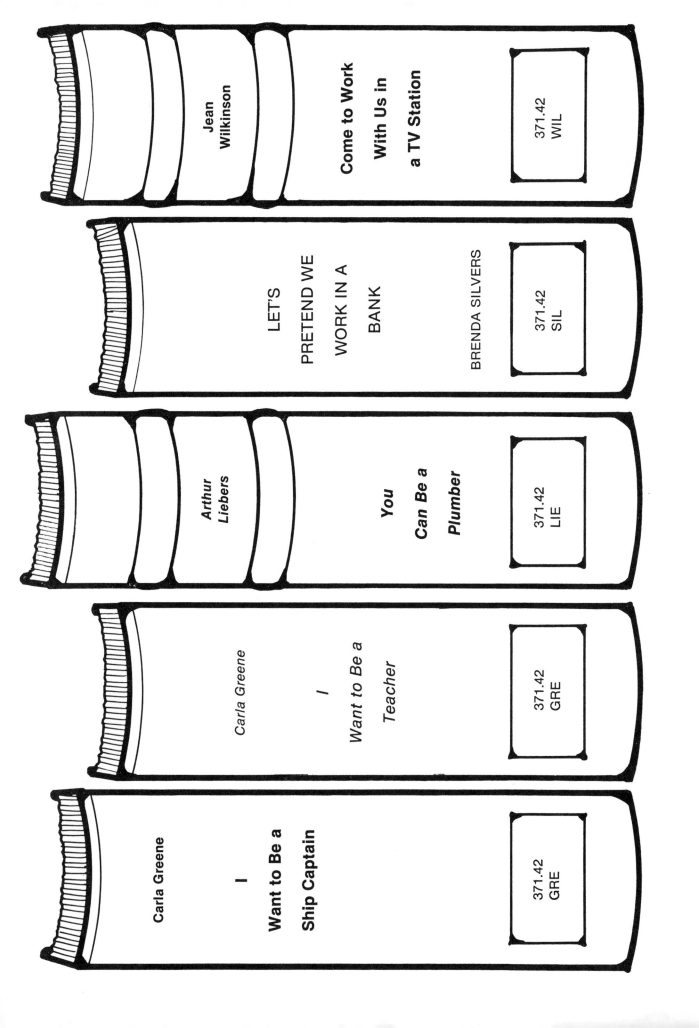

Carla Greene

I
Want to Be a
Ship Captain

371.42
GRE

Carla Greene

I
Want to Be a
Teacher

371.42
GRE

Arthur
Liebers

You
Can Be a
Plumber

371.42
LIE

LET'S
PRETEND WE
WORK IN A
BANK

BRENDA SILVERS

371.42
SIL

Jean
Wilkinson

Come to Work
With Us in
a TV Station

371.42
WIL

Answer Key

Starting from left to right, the correct order of these books is:

    Greene (*I Want to Be a Ship Captain*)—11
    Greene (*I Want to Be a Teacher*)—12
    Liebers—13
    Silvers—14
    Wilkinson—15

SET 4
ARRANGING NONFICTION BOOKS IN ORDER

Checklist of books used—10 titles in set.

1.	500 PAR	Parker, Bertha M.	Science and Us
2.	510 DUM	Dumas, Enoch	Arithmetic Games
3.	513 LAU	Lauber, Patricia	The Story of Numbers
4.	520 ASI	Asimov, Isaac	Satellites in Outer Space
5.	523 BRA	Branley, Franklin M.	Black Holes, White Dwarfs, and Superstars
6.	535 HEA	Healey, Frederick	Light and Color
7.	539 GAI	Gaines, Mathew	Atomic Energy
8.	550 GOE	Goetz, Delia	Tropical Rain Forests
9.	552 WHI	White, Anne T.	All About Rocks and Minerals
10.	568 DAL	Daly, Kathleen N.	Dinosaurs

Different Call Numbers—500s
Arrange in numerical order by call numbers, 500 to 568.

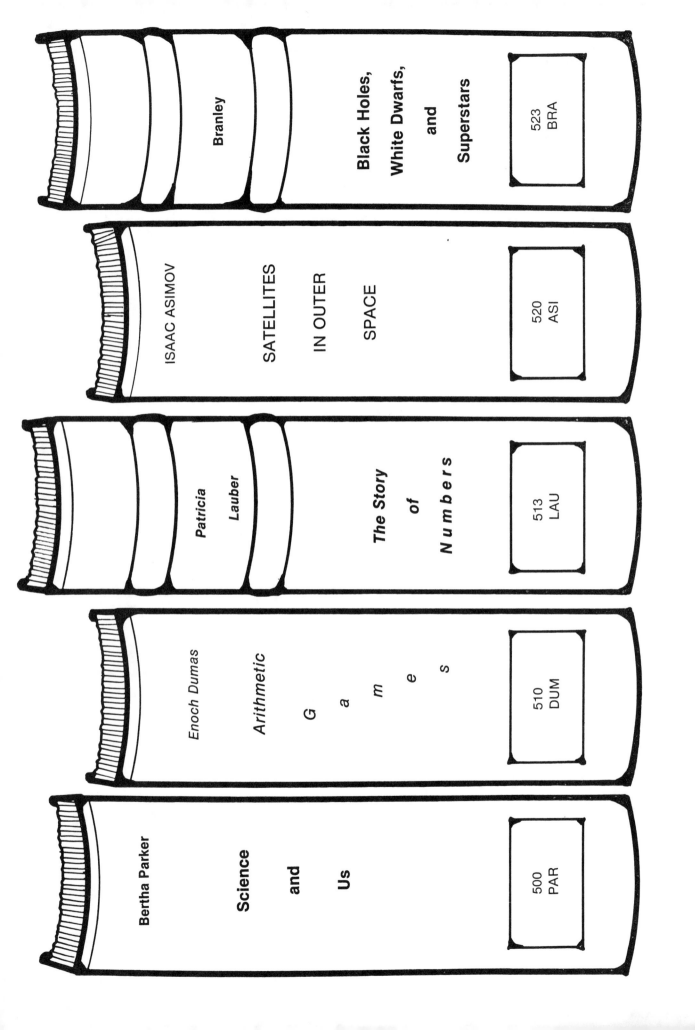

Branley

**Black Holes,
White Dwarfs,
and
Superstars**

523
BRA

ISAAC ASIMOV

SATELLITES

IN OUTER

SPACE

520
ASI

Patricia

Lauber

The Story

of

N u m b e r s

513
LAU

Enoch Dumas

Arithmetic

G

a

m

e

s

510
DUM

Bertha Parker

Science

and

Us

500
PAR

Answer Key

Starting from left to right, the correct order of these books is:

    Parker—1
    Dumas—2
    Lauber—3
    Asimov—4
    Branley—5

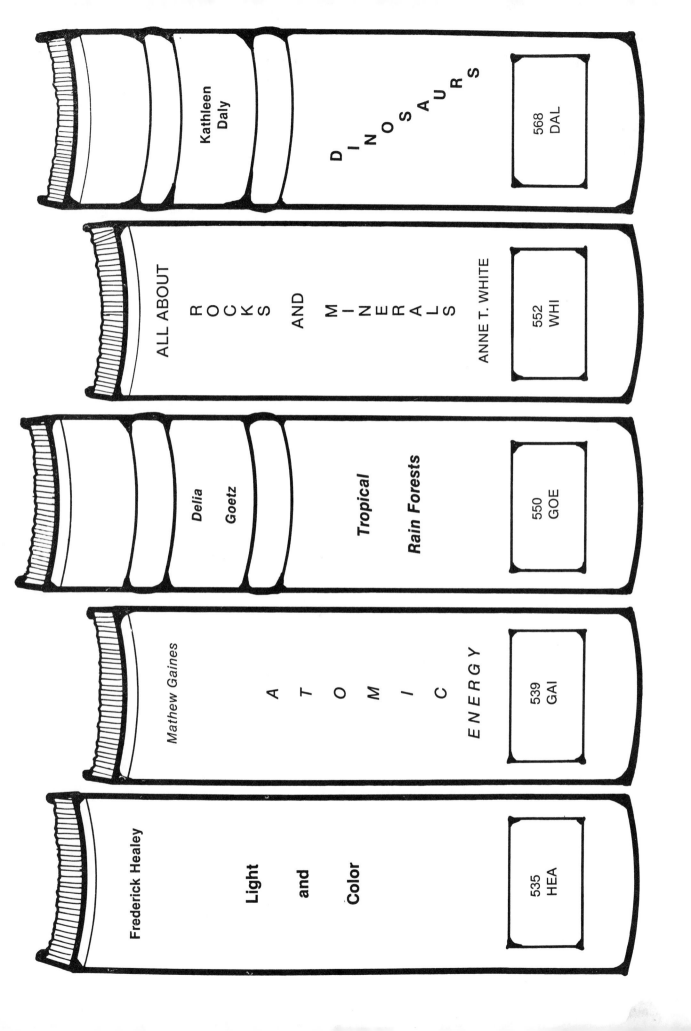

Kathleen
Daly

D
I
N
O
S
A
U
R
S

568
DAL

ALL ABOUT

R
O
C
K
S

AND

M
I
N
E
R
A
L
S

ANNE T. WHITE

552
WHI

Delia

Goetz

Tropical

Rain Forests

550
GOE

Mathew Gaines

A
T
O
M
I
C

ENERGY

539
GAI

Frederick Healey

Light

and

Color

535
HEA

Answer Key

Starting from left to right, the correct order of these books is:

    Healey—6
    Gaines—7
    Goetz—8
    White—9
    Daly—10

SET 5
ARRANGING NONFICTION BOOKS IN ORDER

Checklist of books used — 10 in set.

1.	973 TUN	Tunis, Edwin	Frontier Living
2.	973.1 LAU	Lauber, Patricia	Who Discovered America
3.	973.2 SIE	Siegel, Beatrice	A New Look at the Pilgrims
4.	973.3 BIL	Bliven, Bruce	American Revolution
5.	973.4 AND	Andrist, Ralph K.	To the Pacific With Lewis and Clark
6.	973.5 TIN	Tinkle, Lon	The Valiant Few
7.	973.6 AND	Andrist, Ralph K.	The California Gold Rush
8.	973.7 ELL	Ellis, Keith	The American Civil War
9.	973.8 STA	Stampp, Kenneth	Era of Reconstruction
10.	973.91 COO	Cook, Ann	What Was It Like, When Your Grandparents Were Your Age

Different Call Numbers—973s
Arrange in numerical order by decimal point.

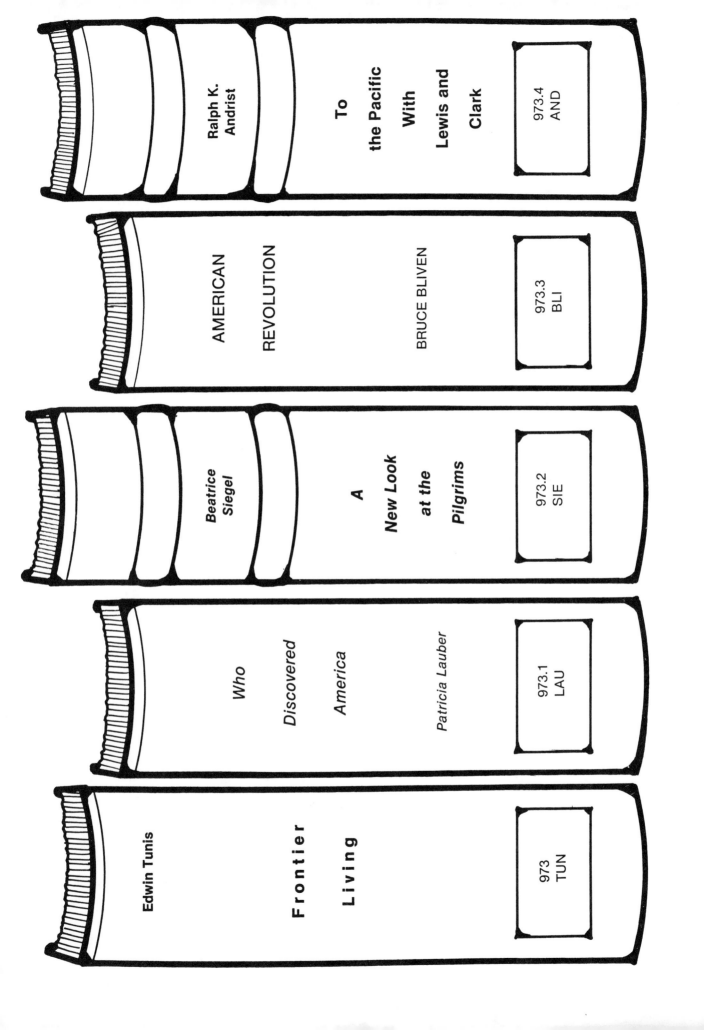

Answer Key

Starting from left to right, the correct order of these books is:
- Tunis—1
- Lauber—2
- Siegel—3
- Bliven—4
- Andrist—5

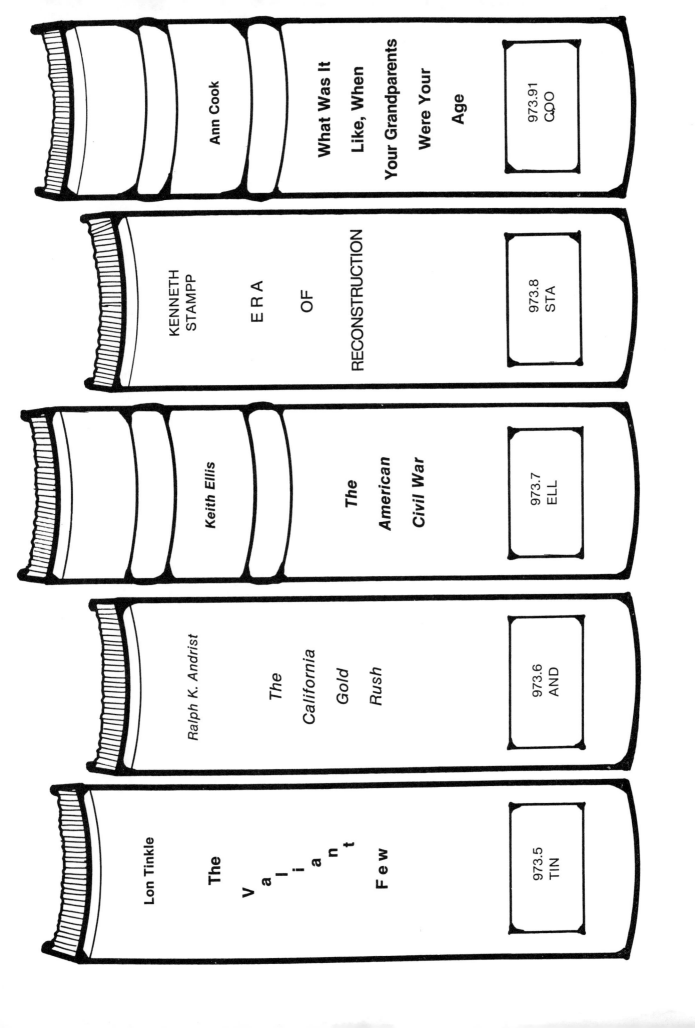

Ann Cook

What Was It
Like, When
Your Grandparents
Were Your
Age

973.91
COO

KENNETH
STAMPP

E R A

OF

RECONSTRUCTION

973.8
STA

Keith Ellis

The
American
Civil War

973.7
ELL

Ralph K. Andrist

The
California
Gold
Rush

973.6
AND

Lon Tinkle

The
V a l i a n t
F e w

973.5
TIN

Answer Key

Starting from left to right, the correct order of these books is:

    Tinkle—6

    Andrist—7

    Ellis—8

    Stampp—9

    Cook—10

SET 6
ARRANGING NONFICTION BOOKS IN ORDER

Checklist of books used — 15 titles in set.

1.	301 JEN	Jennings, Jerry E.	Great Ideas of Man
2.	301.34 RAD	Radlauer, Edward	What Is a Community
3.	330 SHA	Shay, Arthur	What Happens When You Spend Money
4.	333.7 GRE	Green, Ivah	Conservation from A to Z
5.	333.9 GRE	Green, Ivah	Water: Our Most Valuable Natural Resource
6.	352 MIN	Miner, Irene	The True Book of Policemen and Firemen
7.	371.1 HOF	Hoffmann, Elaine	About School Helpers
8.	371.42 BAK	Baker, Eugene	I Want to Be a Bank Teller
9.	380.5 CAI	Cain, Wilma W.	Transportation
10.	383 SCH	Schloat, G. Warren	Adventures of a Letter
11.	385 DAY	Day, John	Trains
12.	387 HOA	Hoare, Robert J.	Travel by Sea
13.	387.7 LEW	Lewellen, John	The True Book of Airports and Airplanes
14.	391 GOR	Gorsline, Douglas	What People Wore
15.	395 PIT	Pitt, Valerie	Let's Find Out About Manners

Different Call Numbers—300s
Arrange in numerical order, 301 to 395.

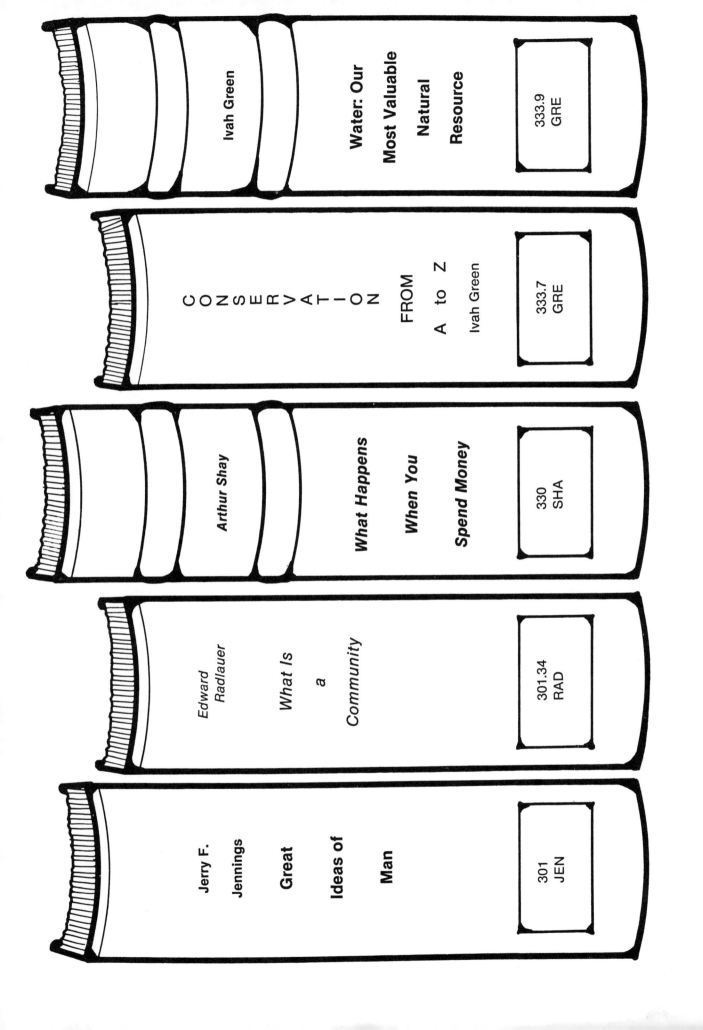

Ivah Green

Water: Our

Most Valuable

Natural

Resource

333.9
GRE

CONSERVATION

FROM

A to Z

Ivah Green

333.7
GRE

Arthur Shay

What Happens

When You

Spend Money

330
SHA

Edward
Radlauer

What Is

a

Community

301.34
RAD

Jerry F.
Jennings

Great

Ideas of

Man

301
JEN

Answer Key

Starting from left to right, the correct order of these books is:

    Jennings—1
    Radlauer—2
    Shay—3
    Green (*Conservation from A to Z*)—4
    Green (*Water: Our Most Valuable Natural Resource*)—5

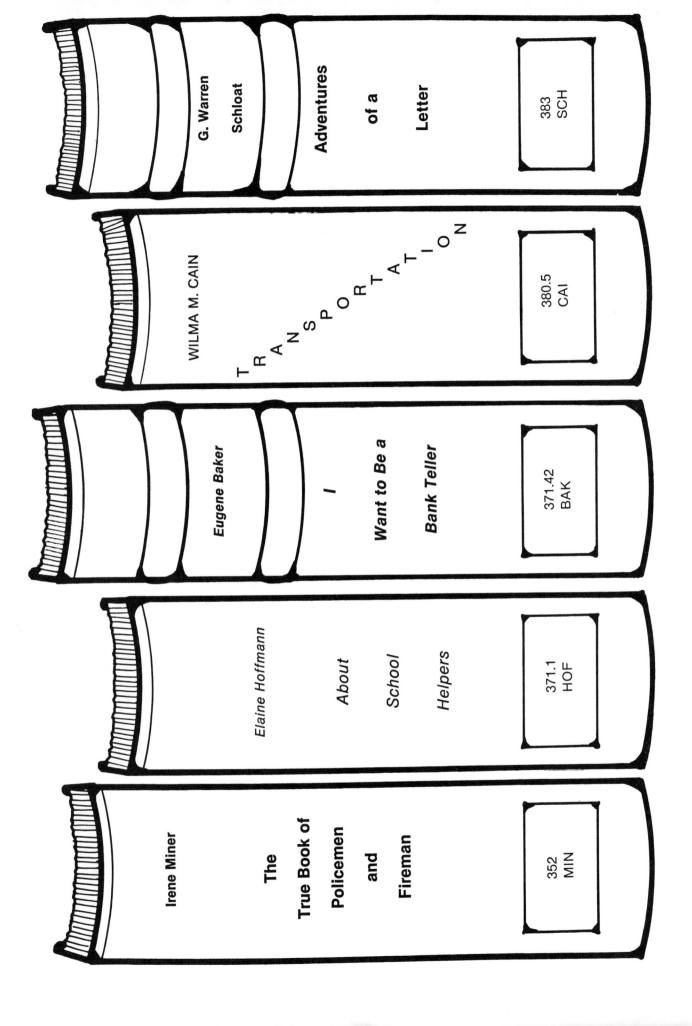

Answer Key

Starting from left to right, the correct order of these books is:
    Miner—6
    Hoffmann—7
    Baker—8
    Cain—9
    Schloat—10

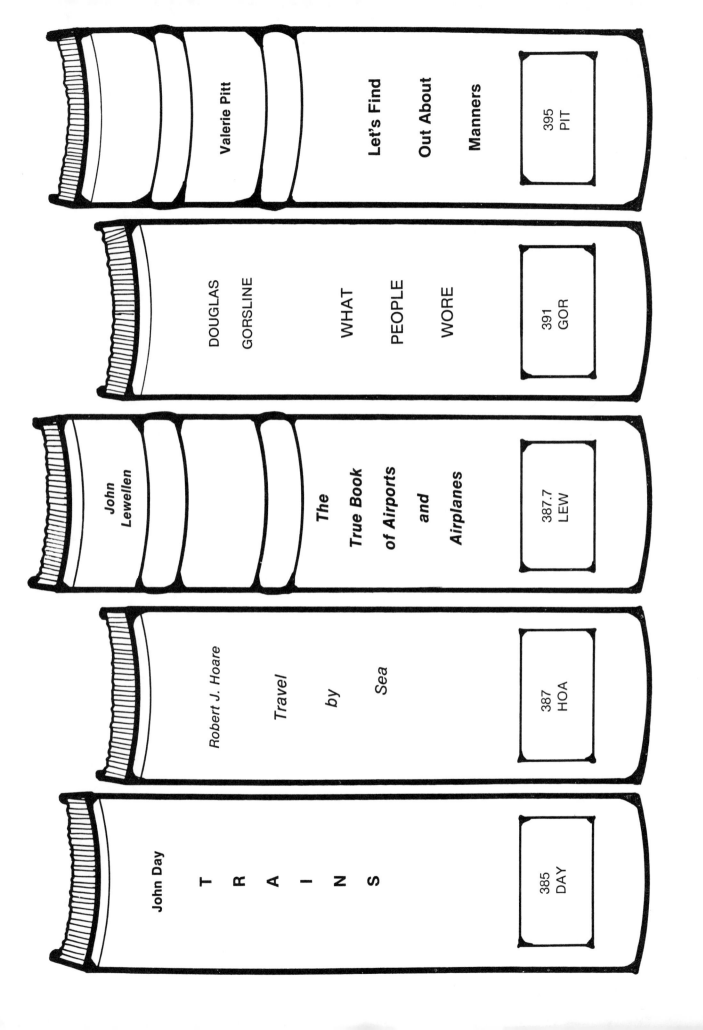

Valerie Pitt

Let's Find Out About Manners

395 PIT

DOUGLAS GORSLINE

WHAT PEOPLE WORE

391 GOR

John Lewellen

The True Book of Airports and Airplanes

387.7 LEW

Robert J. Hoare

Travel by Sea

387 HOA

John Day

TRAINS

385 DAY

Answer Key

Starting from left to right, the correct order of these books is:

    Day—11
    Hoare—12
    Lewellen—13
    Gorsline—14
    Pitt—15

SET 7
ARRANGING NONFICTION BOOKS IN ORDER

Checklist of books used — 15 titles in set.

1.	636 DAR	Darby, Gene	What Is a Chicken
2.	636 LEW	Lewellen, John	True Book of Farm Animals
3.	636 SEL	Selsam, Millicent	Egg to Chick
4.	636.1 DEL	Dell, Catherine	Wonder Book of Horses
5.	636.1 ROB	Roberts, Peter	What Horse Is That?
6.	636.3 WHI	Whitlock, Ralph	Sheep
7.	636.6 ZIM	Zim, Herbert S.	Parakeets
8.	636.7 HEN	Henry, Marguerite	Album of Dogs
9.	636.7 HES	Hess, Lilo	A Puppy for You
10.	636.7 POS	Posell, Elsa	Dogs
11.	636.8 FED	Feder, Jan	Life of a Cat
12.	636.8 PON	Pond, Grace	Family Library of Cats
13.	636.8 SEL	Selsam, Millicent	How Kittens Grow
14.	636.9 SHU	Shuttlesworth, Dorothy	Gerbils and Other Small Pets
15.	636.93 FED	Feder, Jan	Life of a Rabbit

Different Call Numbers—636s
Arrange in numerical order by decimal point.
Some call numbers are the same, so arrange those books by the authors' last names.

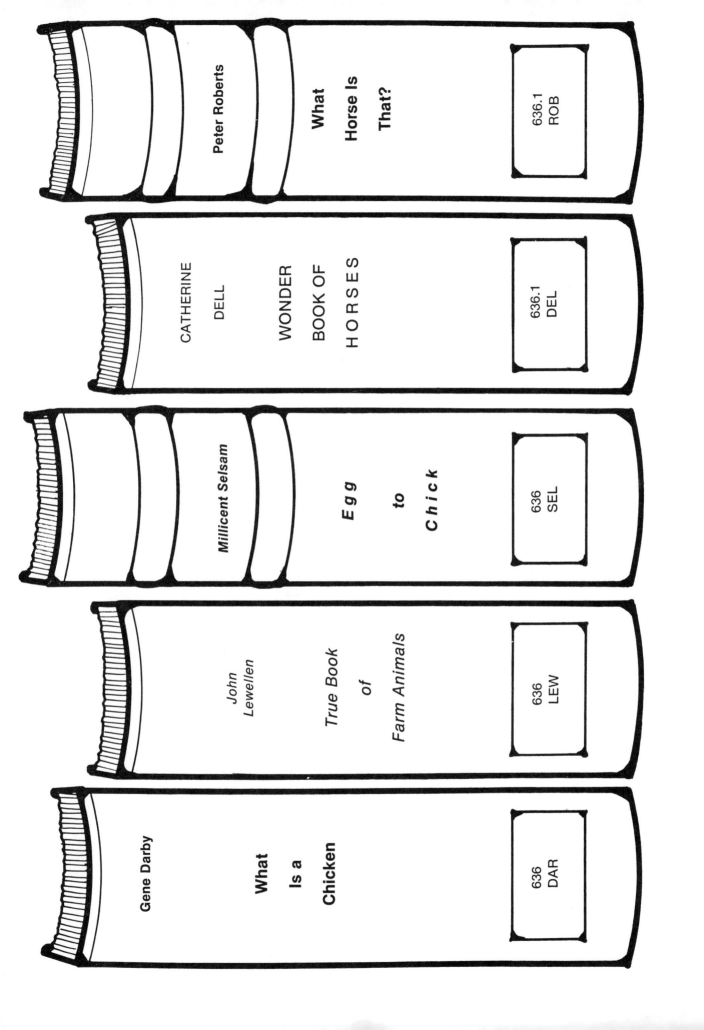

Answer Key

Starting from left to right, the correct order of these books is:

Darby—1
Lewellen—2
Selsam—3
Dell—4
Roberts—5

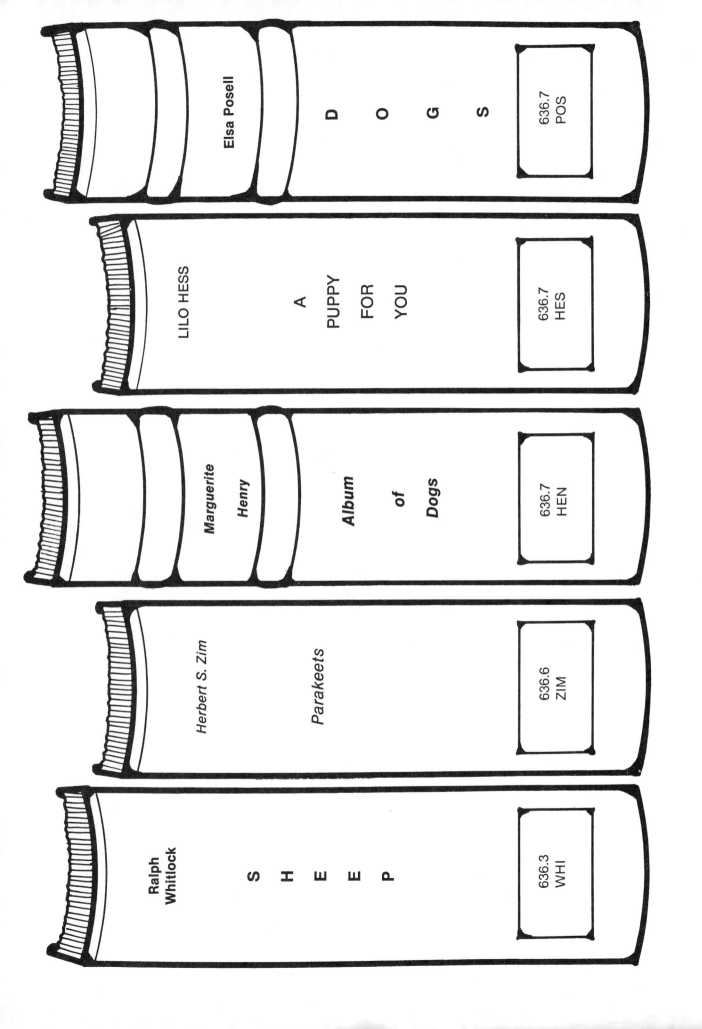

Answer Key

Starting from left to right, the correct order of these books is:

    Whitlock—6

    Zim—7

    Henry—8

    Hess—9

    Posell—10

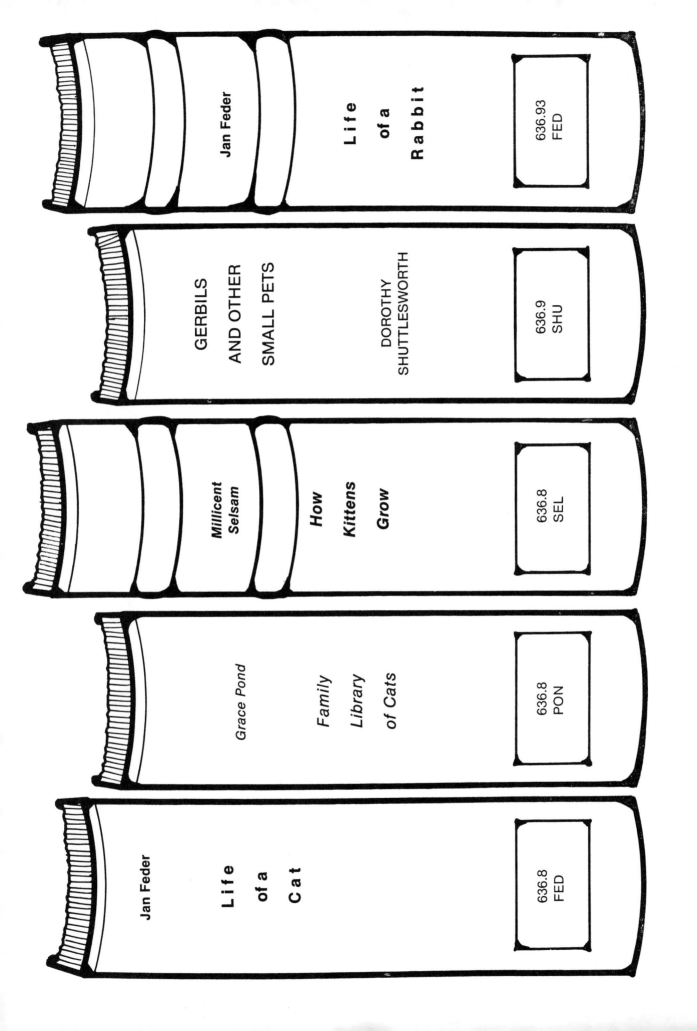

Jan Feder
Life of a Rabbit
636.93
FED

GERBILS AND OTHER SMALL PETS
DOROTHY SHUTTLESWORTH
636.9
SHU

Millicent Selsam
How Kittens Grow
636.8
SEL

Grace Pond
Family Library of Cats
636.8
PON

Jan Feder
Life of a Cat
636.8
FED

Answer Key

Starting from left to right, the correct order of these books is:
    Feder—11
    Pond—12
    Selsam—13
    Shuttlesworth—14
    Feder—15

SET 8
ARRANGING NONFICTION BOOKS IN ORDER

Checklist of books used — 10 in set.

1.	921 ARN DEL	Benedict Arnold, Hero and Traitor	Author — De Leeuw
2.	921 CLA MAY	Bobby Clarke, Hockey With a Grin	Author — May
3.	921 EDI THO	Edison the Inventor	Author — Thomson
4.	921 KEN WHI	Meet John F. Kennedy	Author — White
5.	921 MOR HAY	Samuel Morse and the Electronic Age	Author — Hays
6.	921 NIG HUM	Florence Nightingale	Author — Hume
7.	921 PAS PAI	Louis Pasteur	Author — Pain
8.	921 STE PEA	Robert Louis Stevenson	Author — Peare
9.	921 TUB PET	Harriet Tubman: Conductor of the Underground Railroad	Author — Petry
10.	921 VER BOR	Jules Verne: the Man Who Invented the Future	Author — Born

Call Number 921 — BIOGRAPHY
Arrange by the last name of the *PERSON* the book is about.

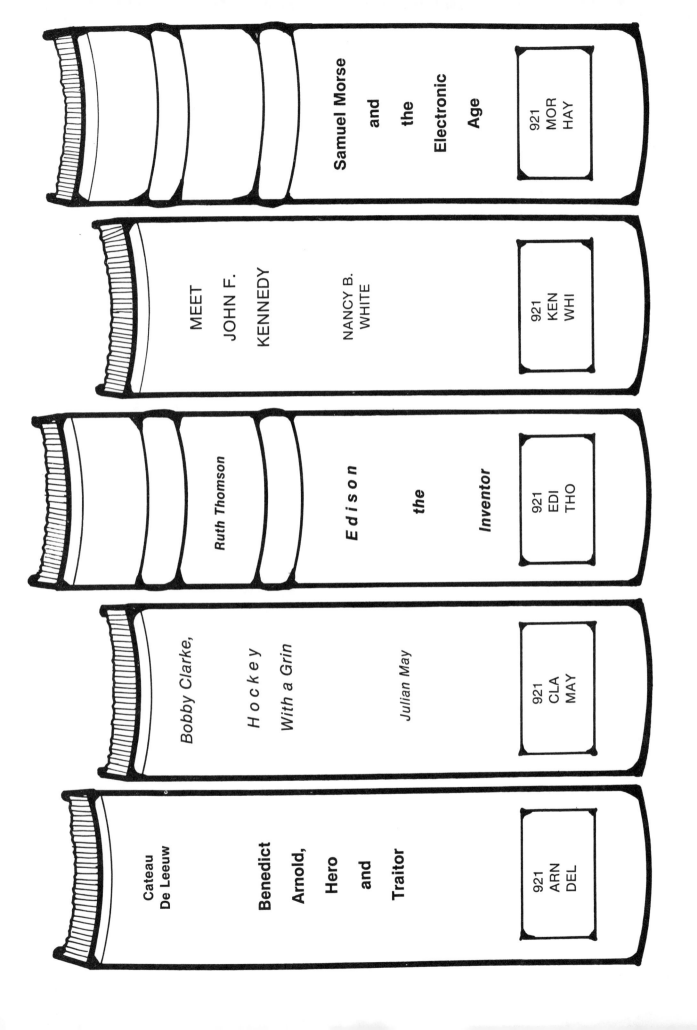

Answer Key

Starting from left to right, the correct order of these books is:

    De Leeuw—1

    May—2

    Thomson—3

    White—4

    Hays—5

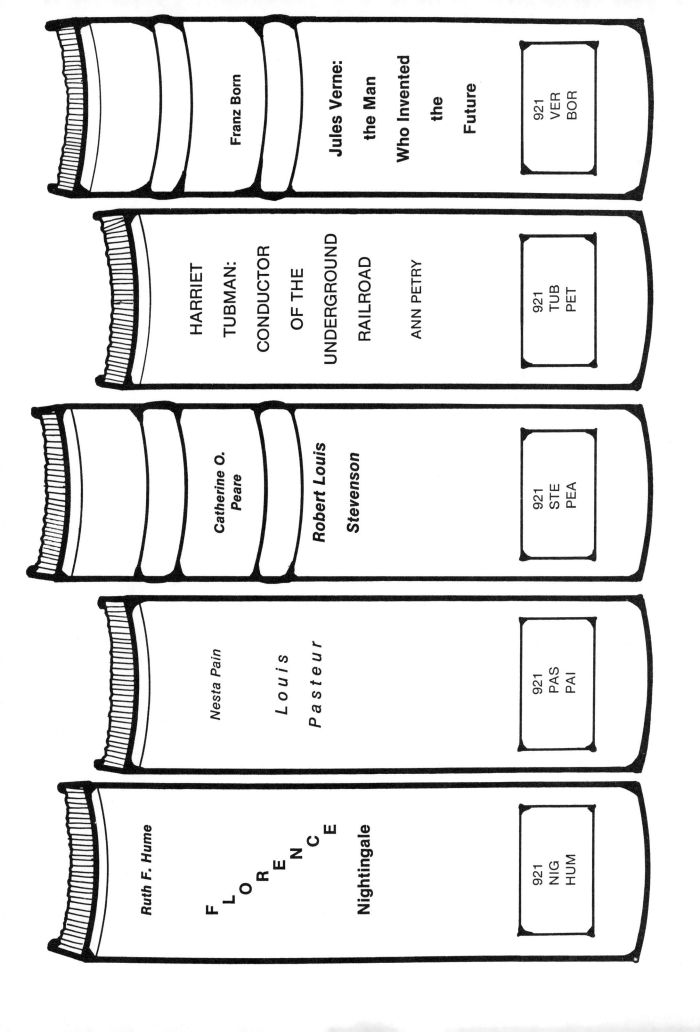

Franz Born

Jules Verne:
the Man
Who Invented
the
Future

921
VER
BOR

HARRIET
TUBMAN:
CONDUCTOR
OF THE
UNDERGROUND
RAILROAD

ANN PETRY

921
TUB
PET

Catherine O.
Peare

Robert Louis
Stevenson

921
STE
PEA

Nesta Pain

Louis
Pasteur

921
PAS
PAI

Ruth F. Hume

F
L
O
R
E
N
C
E

Nightingale

921
NIG
HUM

Answer Key

Starting from left to right, the correct order of these books is:

    Hume—6
    Pain—7
    Peare—8
    Petry—9
    Born—10

SET 9
ARRANGING NONFICTION BOOKS IN ORDER

Checklist of books used — 15 in set.

1. 921 ALE GUN — Alexander the Great — Author — Gunther

2. 921 BAN SHA — Frederick Banting — Author — Shaw

3. 921 BEL PET — Alexander Graham Bell — Author — Petrie

4. 921 CAR WHI — George Washington Carver; the Story of a Great American — Author — White

5. 921 EAT BAS — Timothy Eaton — Author — Bassett

6. 921 HUL HUN — Bobby Hull — Author — Hunt

7. 921 HUL ZAL — Bobby Hull, the Golden Jet — Author — Zalewski

8. 921 KEL PEA — The Helen Keller Story — Author — Pearce

9. 921 LIN BRA — Abe Lincoln the Young Years — Author — Brandt

10. 921 LIN THO — Abraham Lincoln — Author — Thomas

11. 921 LIN WAL — No Luck for Lincoln — Author — Walters

12. 921 OCO BEN — Justice Sandra Day O'Connor — Author — Bentley

13. 921 SCH MAN — The Story of Albert Schweitzer — Author — Manton

	921	
14.	SIT	Sitting Bull, the Story of an American Indian
	KNO	Author — Knoop

	921	
15.	WON	Picture Life of Stevie Wonder
	EDW	Author — Edwards

Call Number 921 — BIOGRAPHY

Arrange by the last name of the *PERSON* the book is about.

Arrange by authors' last names if there is more than one book written about the same person.

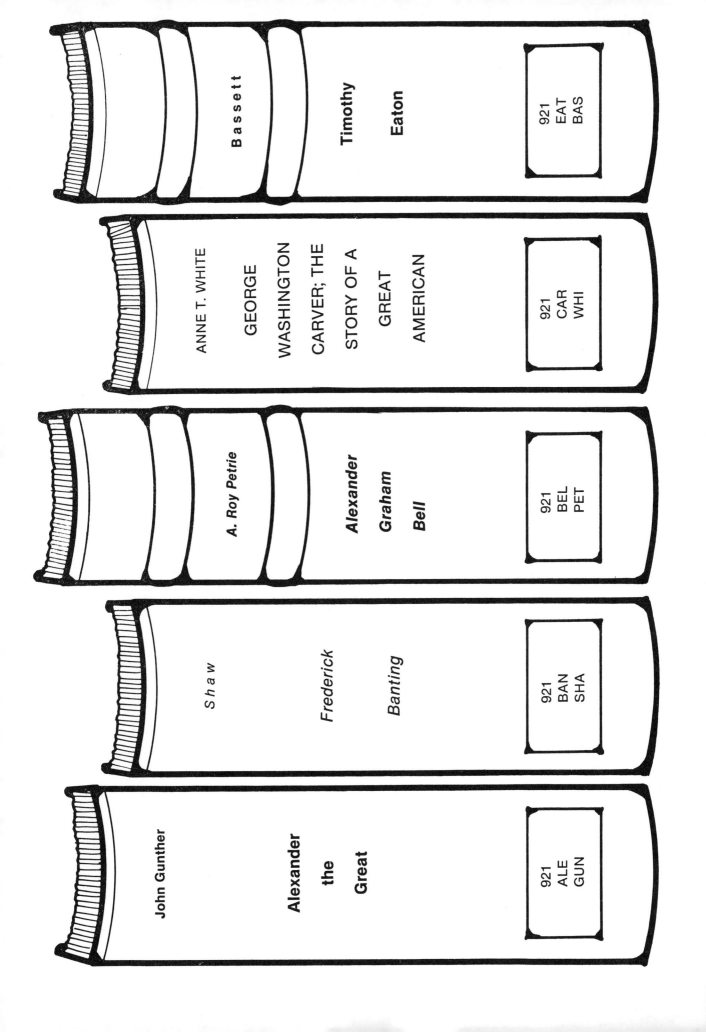

Answer Key

Starting from left to right, the correct order of these books is:
    Gunther—1
    Shaw—2
    Petrie—3
    White—4
    Bassett—5

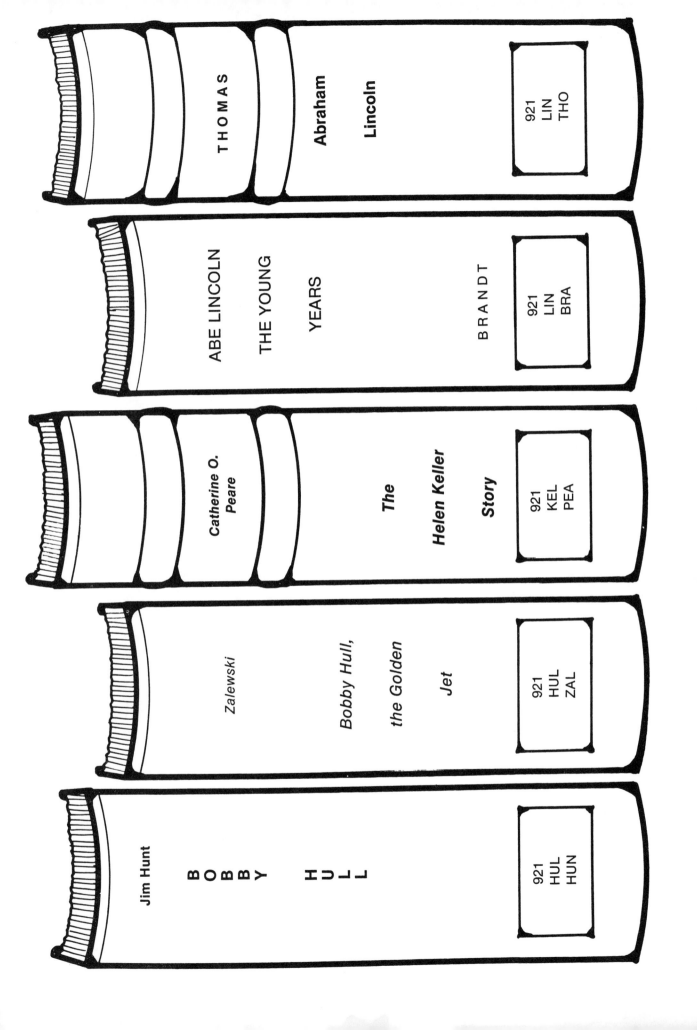

Answer Key

Starting from left to right, the correct order of these books is:

    Hunt—6
    Zalewski—7
    Peare—8
    Brandt—9
    Thomas—10

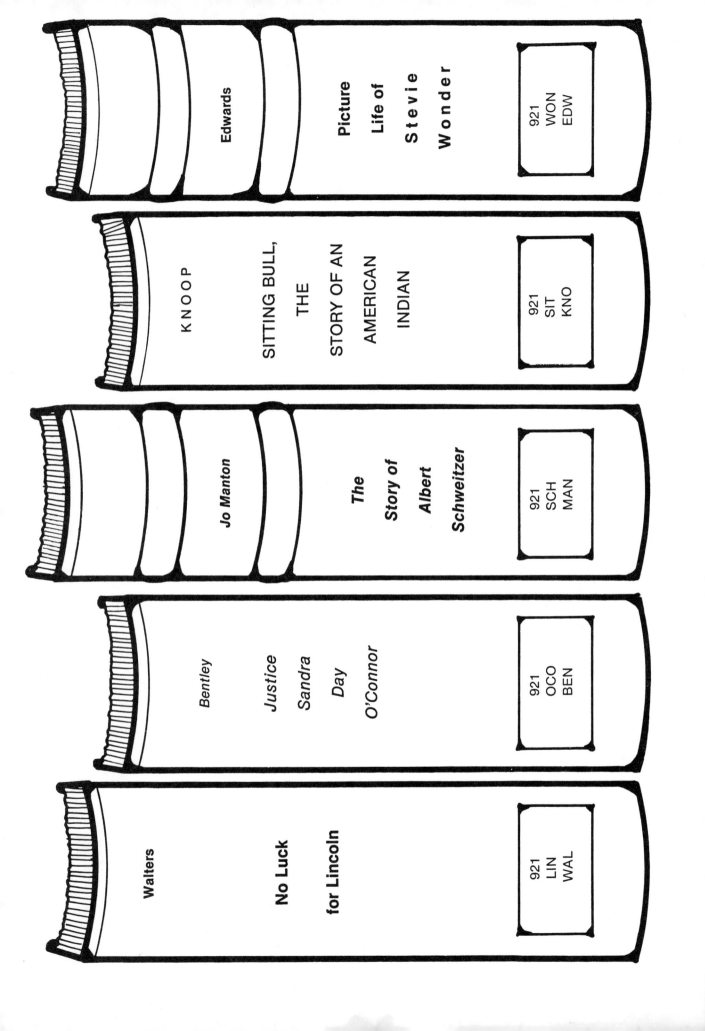

Answer Key

Starting from left to right, the correct order of these books is:
    Walters—11
    Bentley—12
    Manton—13
    Knoop—14
    Edwards—15

SET 10
ARRANGING NONFICTION BOOKS IN ORDER

Checklist of books used — 15 titles in set.

1.	791 KRA	Kramer, Ann	Stuntmen and Daredevils
2.	793.7 AND	Anderson, V.	Thinking Games Book
3.	793.8 KET	Kettlekamp, Larry	Magic Made Easy
4.	794.1 LAN	Langfield, Paul	Chess
5.	796 DOL	Dolan, Edward	Calling the Play
6.	796.2 ROD	Roddick, Dan	Frisbee Disc Basics
7.	796.21 OLN	Olney, Ross R.	Roller Skating!!
8.	796.34 SUL	Sullivan, George	Better Basketball for Boys
9.	796.34 BOC	Boccaccio, Tony	Racquetball Basics
10.	796.4 SUL	Sullivan, George	Better Gymnastics for Girls
11.	796.6 EVA	Evans, Ken	Cycling
12.	796.7 RAD	Radlauer, Edward	Wild Wheels
13.	796.96 OLN	Olney, Ross R.	Super-Champions of Ice Hockey
14.	797.21 DUF	Duffy, Tony	Swimming and Diving
15.	798.2 GRE	Green, Carol	Let's Ride

Different Call Numbers—790s
Arrange in numerical order by call numbers, 791 to 798.2.
If the first part of the call number is the same, arrange the books by decimal point.

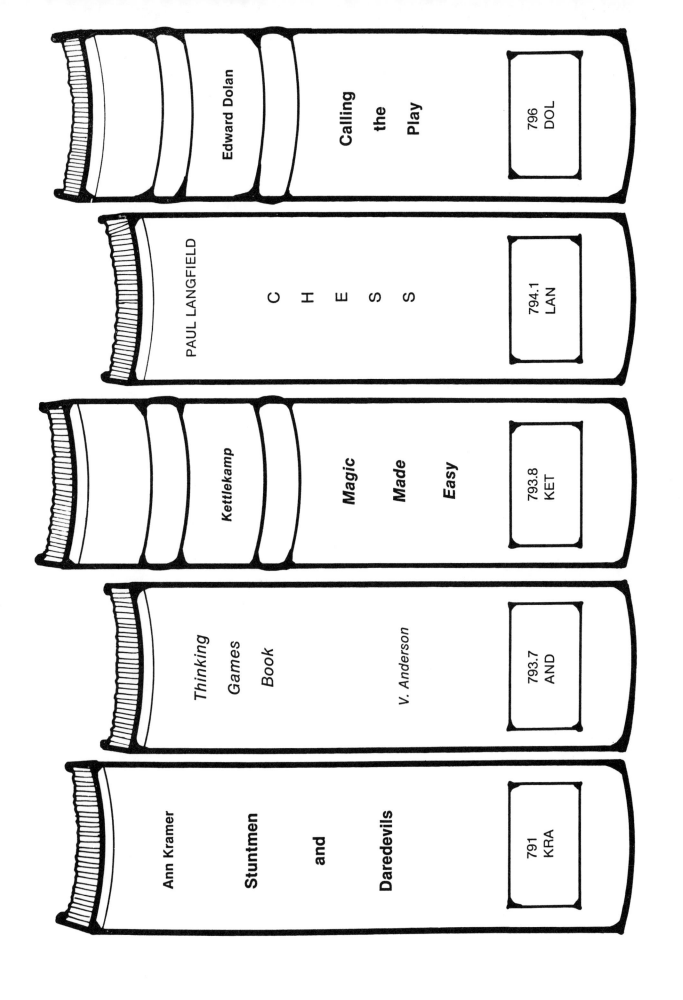

Edward Dolan

Calling

the

Play

796
DOL

PAUL LANGFIELD

C

H

E

S

S

794.1
LAN

Kettlekamp

Magic

Made

Easy

793.8
KET

Thinking

Games

Book

V. Anderson

793.7
AND

Ann Kramer

Stuntmen

and

Daredevils

791
KRA

Answer Key

Starting from left to right, the correct order of these books is:

    Kramer—1
    Anderson—2
    Kettlekamp—3
    Langfield—4
    Dolan—5

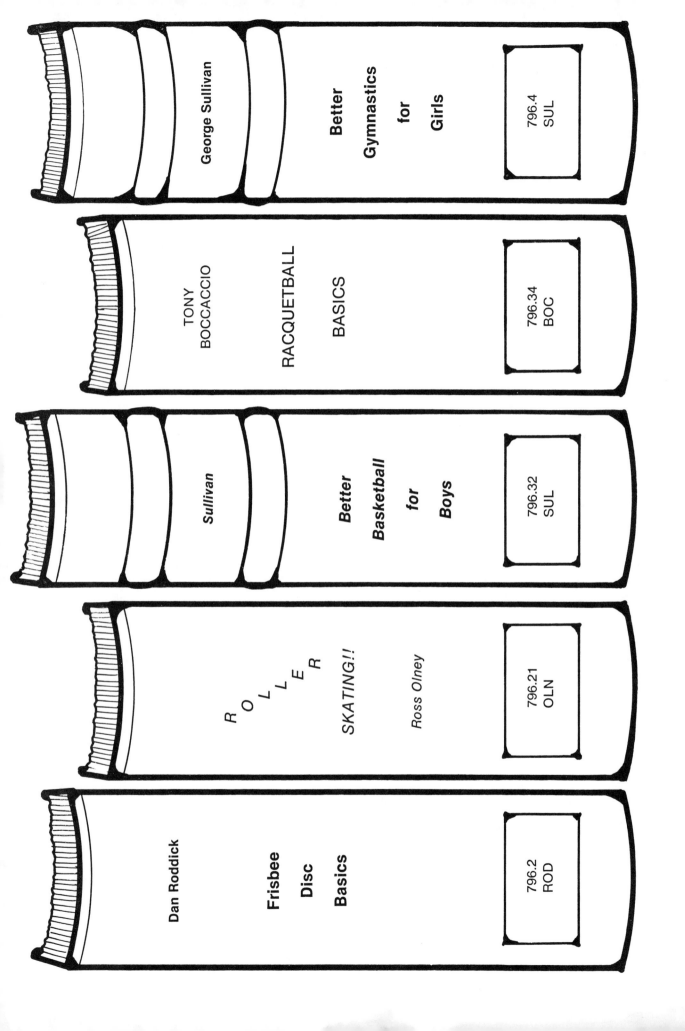

Answer Key

Starting from left to right, the correct order of these books is:
Roddick—6
Olney—7
Sullivan (*Better Basketball for Boys*)—8
Boccaccio—9
Sullivan (*Better Gymnastics for Girls*)—10

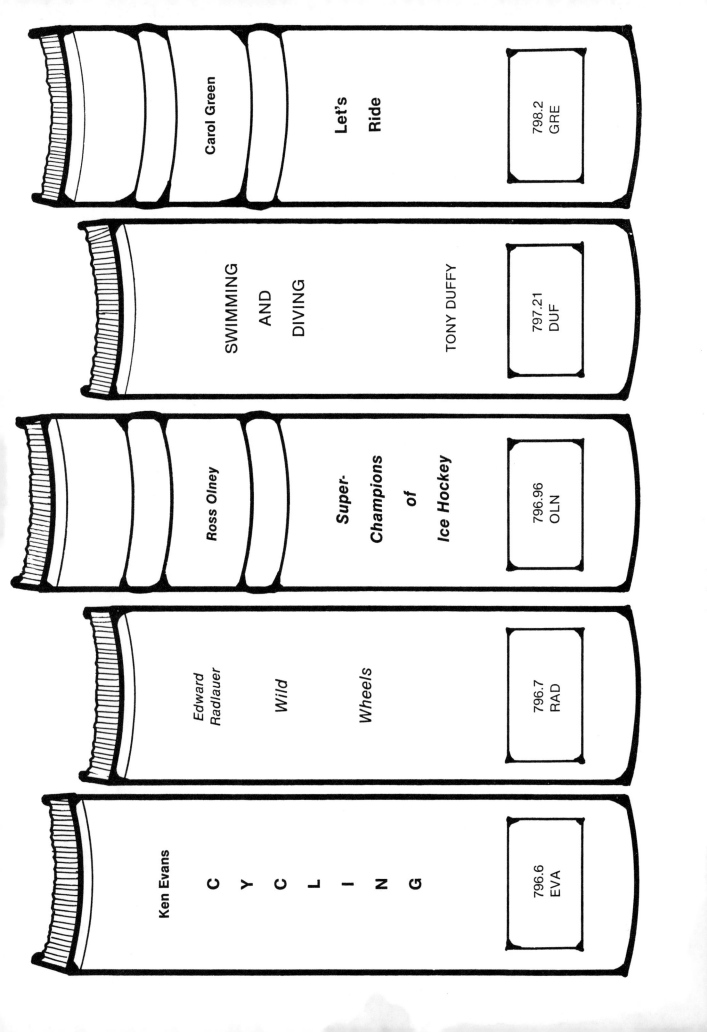

Answer Key

Starting from left to right, the correct order of these books is:

Evans—11

Radlauer—12

Olney—13

Duffy—14

Green—15

Bookends

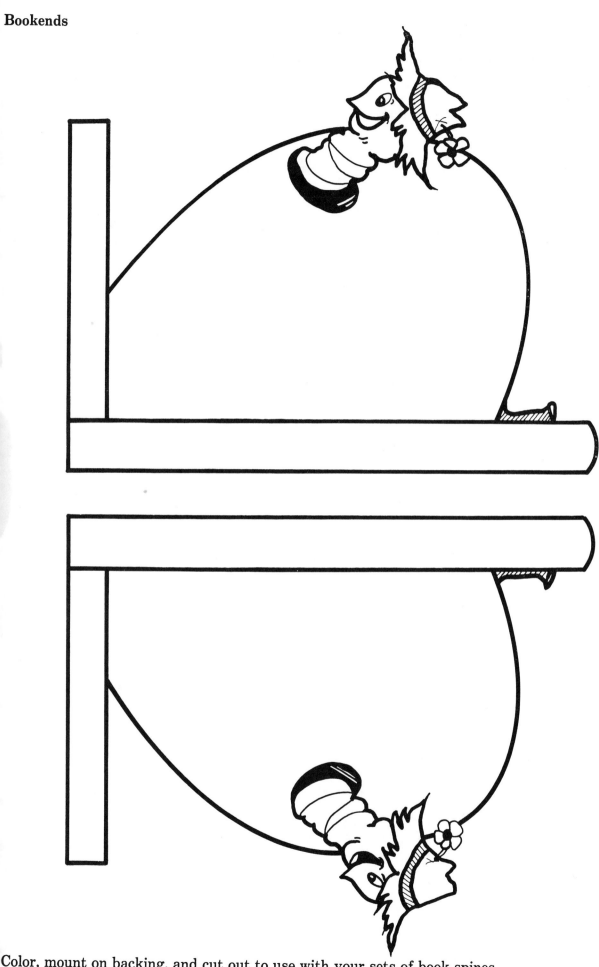

Color, mount on backing, and cut out to use with your sets of book spines.